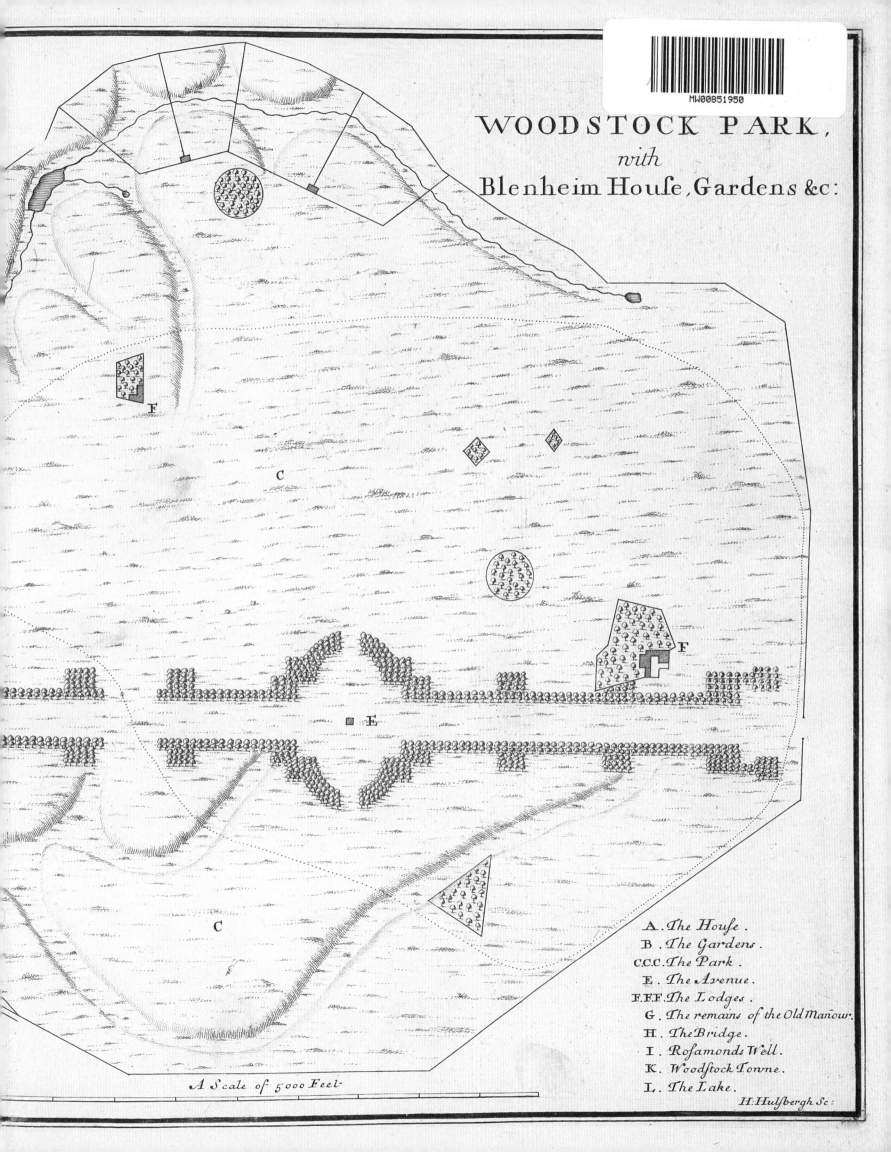

WOODSTOCK PARK,
with
Blenheim House, Gardens &c:

F

F

F

C

E

C

A . *The Houfe* .
B . *The Gardens* .
C.C.C. *The Park* .
E . *The Avenue* .
F.F.F. *The Lodges* .
G . *The remains of the Old Manour* .
H . *The Bridge* .
I . *Rofamonds Well* .
K . *Woodftock Towne* .
L . *The Lake* .

A Scale of 5000 Feet

H. Hulfbergh Sc:

BLENHEIM

*300 YEARS OF LIFE
IN A PALACE*

Photography by Hugo Rittson-Thomas

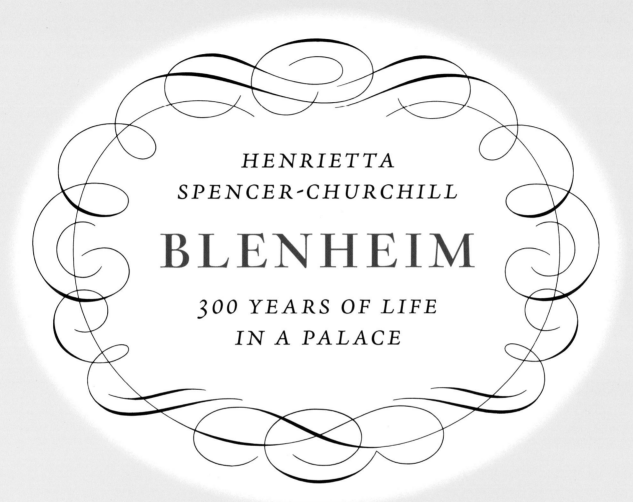

HENRIETTA
SPENCER-CHURCHILL

BLENHEIM

*300 YEARS OF LIFE
IN A PALACE*

with Alexandra Parsons

RIZZOLI
NEW YORK

New York · Paris · London · Milan

First published in the United States of America in 2024 by
Rizzoli International Publications, Inc.
300 Park Avenue South, New York, NY 10010

www.rizzoliusa.com

Copyright © Henrietta Spencer-Churchill

Publisher: Charles Miers
Editor: Ellen Nidy
Design: Robert Dalrymple
Production Manager: Barbara Sadick
Managing Editor: Lynn Scrabis

Printed in Singapore

2024 2025 2026 2027 2028 / 10 9 8 7 6 5 4 3 2 1

ISBN: 978-0-8478-3350-4

Library of Congress Control Number: 2024783972

Visit us online:
Facebook.com / RizzoliNewYork
instagram.com/rizzolibooks
twitter.com/Rizzoli_Books
pinterest.com/rizzolibooks
youtube.com/user/RizzoliNY
issuu.com/rizzoli

All original photograpy by Hugo Rittson-Thomas other than below
Alamy: page 233
Blenheim Archives: pages 48/49, 70/71, 72, 76, 81, 108, 146, 147, 148, 149, 188,
263 top, 268/269, 280/281, 282/283, 285, 291,292, 303, 306/307, 318, 319
Blenheim Albums: pages 40, 41, 56 bottom, 87, 270/271
Blenheim Art Foundation: pages 334/345, 346/347
Blenheim International Horse Trials: page 350
The Bodleian Library: pages 63, 64/65
Bridgeman Library: pages 44, 252 top, 338
Churchill Archives Centre: page 33
Future Content (*Country Life*): pages 86, 189
National Portrait Gallery, London: pages 18, 28, 29 top, 31, 37, 60, 61
Pete Seaward Photography: pages 2/3, 4/5, 16/17, 19, 20, 21, 22, 23 left,
24, 25, 26, 27, 32, 36, 38, 39, 46/47, 50/51, 68, 78, 84, 92/93, 94/95, 97, 100/101,
106/107, 174/175, 176, 204/205, 206/207, 217, 238/239, 248/249, 250/251, 253,
254/255, 264/265, 296/297, 308 bottom left, 310/311, 316, 317, 330/331
332, 339, 340/341, 348/349, 352/353, 354/355
RIBA: page 210
Royal Academy: page 223
Victoria & Albert Museum: page 273
Wiki Commons: page 236

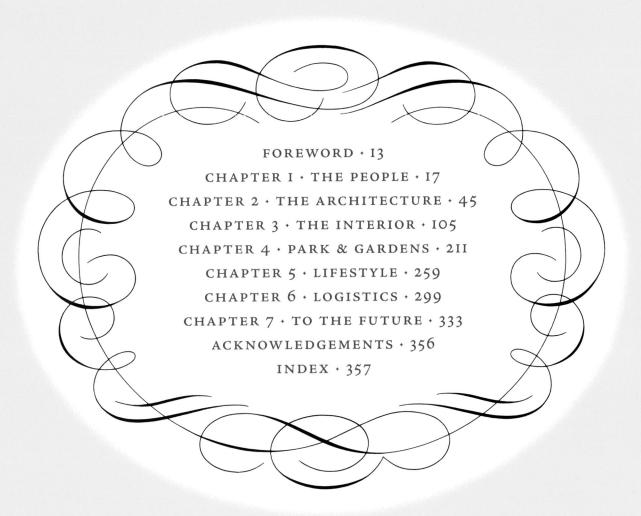

FOREWORD

In a celebrated thought experiment, the philosopher Thomas Hobbes invited his readers to imagine a ship. Over time, the wood forming the deck, mast, jib and hull wore out and had to be replaced. Eventually, not one plank from the original ship survived. To the casual observer, the ship appeared no different from the day it had first taken to sea. Was it still, asked Hobbes, the same vessel, even though no element of the original remained?

A stately home such as Blenheim is a little like Hobbes's ship. The façades, porticos, courtyards and colonnades are almost exactly as the palace's creators, John and Sarah Churchill, would have known them three centuries ago. Yet from almost the moment the palace was occupied, stones were being repaired, timbers were being replaced, paintwork was being touched up and roofs were being patched. There is little at Blenheim today that hasn't felt the joiner's plane, the mason's chisel, the plaster's trowel or the welder's torch over the past three hundred years. The instagrammer with the selfie-stick in the twenty-first century nevertheless sees the same prodigious confection of pinnacles, towers, ornaments and trophies that stupefied onlookers in the age of Walpole, Pope and Swift.

Every Duke and Duchess of Marlborough since John and Sarah Churchill have been site managers, building inspectors and quantity surveyors at least as much as they have been peers of the realm and great persons in the land. It is this double-handed role that *Blenheim: 300 Years of Life in a Palace* sets out in magnificent style. My mother, Henrietta Spencer-Churchill, is singularly placed to describe how Blenheim's occupants across the centuries have managed, glorified and revitalised this extraordinary house, which serves a unique role as private dwelling, princely seat and national war memorial.

Having grown up in Blenheim, my mother is familiar with almost every inch of the building, from the statues gracing the roofline to the flagstones lining the cellars. She knows how each generation of the Churchill family has left its mark – subtly or ostentatiously, triumphantly or ruinously – on the palace. She is acutely aware of the demands the care of such a monumental edifice can make of the custodian, both financial and emotional. She apprehends, too, that life in a house like Blenheim

has been sustained as much by those whose names appear only in receipt books or on pay rolls as those celebrated in portraits on the walls. This book gives such individuals their due.

My mother has also pursued a highly successful career as an interior designer, in the United Kingdom, the United States and across the world. While some interior designers will swoop in only once the builders have wrapped up their dustsheets, my mother likes to be there, in hard hat and hi-vis jacket, from the moment the foreman takes charge, sometimes before the contractors have even brewed their first pot of tea. As a result, she knows exactly what is involved in almost every aspect of construction, maintenance and decoration.

At Blenheim, she has combined her heritage and her vocation. For decades, she has helped oversee the continuous round of works that are the daily reality of life in the palace, whether they involve recarpeting a corridor, rehanging a set of pictures, replacing a roof or repurposing an entire block. She has applied her exceptional knowledge of Blenheim's history, developments in architecture, and the marketplace of arts and antiques in the service of this task, ensuring that nothing is incongruous, yet also that nothing tends towards impracticality or pastiche. One of the great values of *Blenheim: 300 Years of Life in a Palace* is its exposure of how this work is done and what can be achieved through subtle interventions.

Blenheim has from the moment John Vanburgh plotted out its dimensions inspired great artwork. One need only glance at the painted ceiling in the Great Hall or Louis Laguerre's whimsical murals in the Saloon for a sense of how the palace has animated artistic minds. Hugo Rittson-Thomas adds to this corpus with the photographs he has taken for the book, which capture the romantic vision of Vanburgh and the garden designer Capability Brown as few others have done.

The forces of renewal and preservation have been in friction at Blenheim since the day the cornerstone was set. *Blenheim: 300 Years of Life in a Palace* documents in exquisite detail how that tension has ultimately proved to be creative.

Dr David Gelber, PhD

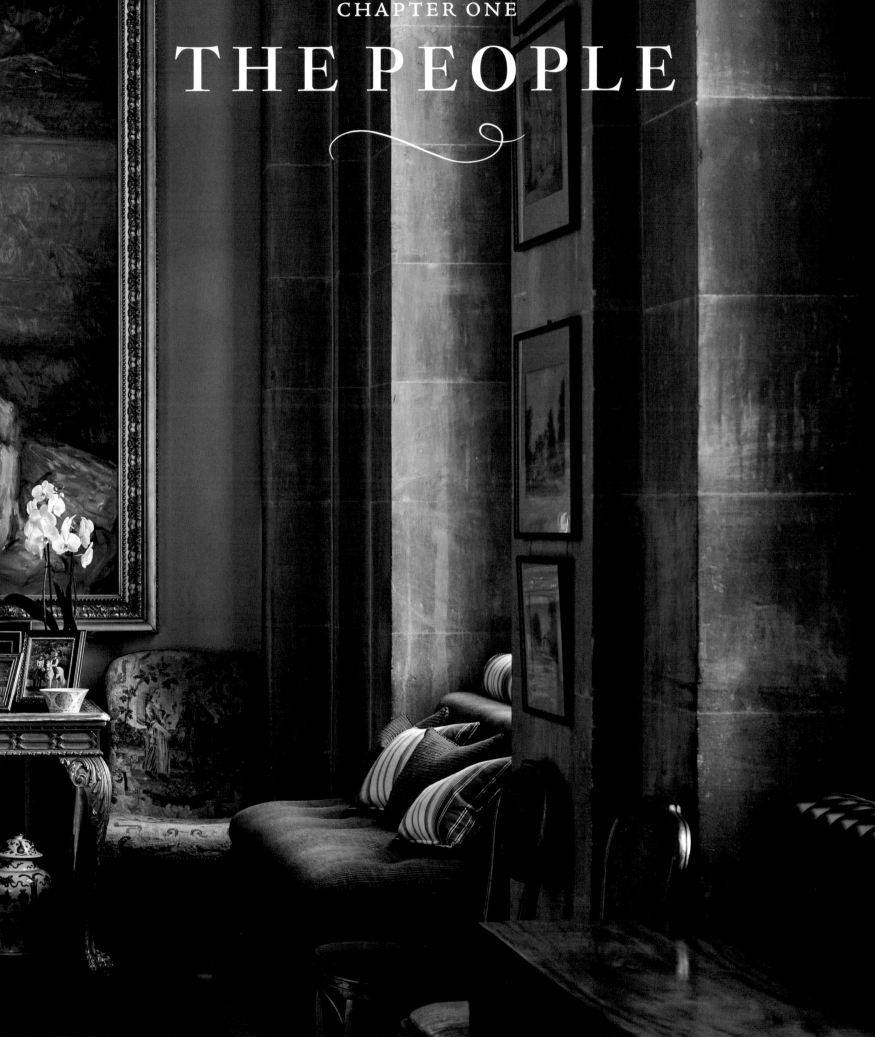

CHAPTER ONE

THE PEOPLE

THE PEOPLE

Just one family have lived, loved, squabbled, partied, plotted, laughed, cried and indulged in passions artistic, scientific, horticultural and theatrical under the three-acre roof of Blenheim Palace for the past 320 years… and that is my family, the descendants of John Churchill, 1st Duke of Marlborough and his redoubtable Duchess, Sarah.

previous pages Myself and my border terrier, Bruno, sitting under one of my favourite portraits of my great-grand-mother Consuleo Vanderbilt, painted by Umberto Veruda in 1903.

left This life-size painting by John Closterman was commissioned for the Churchill family home at St. Albans. The Duke is seated on the left; the youngest child, Lady Mary, is at his feet playing with a spaniel. Lady Elizabeth is between her parents; the Duchess reaches to the eldest daughter, Henrietta; Lady Anne in red picks orange blossom; and the young Marquess of Blandford (who died in childhood) completes the group. By the time John and Sarah moved into Blenheim, their two surviving children, Henrietta and Mary, were married and had settled elsewhere, and their grandchildren from their daughter Anne were in the erratic care of their father, Charles Spencer.

JOHN, IST DUKE OF MARLBOROUGH

opposite Born in 1650, John Churchill was the son of Winston, a modest West Country landowner and staunch Royalist, and his wife, Elizabeth, who hailed from a family of dour Puritan Parliamentarians. John Churchill learned how to be diplomatic very early on in a fulfilling life during which he would be crowned with the highest military and political accolades that Queen and Country could bestow.

SARAH, IST DUCHESS OF MARLBOROUGH

below Undoubtedly the power behind the Marlborough line, Sarah was a force to be reckoned with. In her own right she became the wealthiest woman in Britain, and she had the foresight to protect the future of Blenheim for generations to come.

Lady Henrietta Churchill
Eldest Daughter to John
Duke of Marlborough by
Sarah his Dutchess.

Lady Anne
Churchill Dau
ghter to John Duke
of Marlborough by
Sarah his Dutchess

The Family of the 1st Duke & Duchess

Henrietta never lived at Blenheim as her mother outlived her. Mother and daughter fell out spectacularly over Henrietta's affair with the poet and playwright William Congreve. The couple were hardly discreet: she went to live with him in Bath and bore him a daughter named Mary, in 1723. Henrietta and her mother were never reconciled.

ANNE, COUNTESS OF SUNDERLAND

below left Anne was her father's favourite child and the most politically active. Like her mother, she held the office of Lady of the Bedchamber to Queen Anne. She married Charles Spencer, Earl of Sunderland, but died young in 1716 leaving five children who were eventually cared for by her mother. Her second eldest son, Charles Spencer, became the 3rd Duke of Marlborough.

LADY ELIZABETH, COUNTESS OF BRIDGEWATER

below center Allegedly the prettiest of Marlborough's four daughters, Lady Elizabeth married the Duke of Bridgewater. A rival portrait painter to Godfrey Kneller, Charles Jervas, claimed to be in love with Lady Elizabeth, who became his template for many other portraits of society ladies. As Horace Walpole noted, "many a homely dame was delighted to find her picture resemble Lady Bridgewater."

HENRIETTA AND ANNE

opposite The two sisters as children in 1691. Henrietta would have been ten and Anne seven. Henrietta died without leaving a male heir. It was Anne who provided Blenheim with the next duke.

HENRIETTA, 2ND DUCHESS OF MARLBOROUGH

above The unfortunate death of sixteen-year-old John in 1703, the Churchill's only surviving son, necessitated an Act of Parliament to allow his daughters and their heirs to inherit the dukedom. Henrietta duly inherited the title upon her father's death, but not Blenheim, which was left to her mother for her lifetime.

LADY MARY, DUCHESS OF MONTAGU

below right Mary was a Court Official, appointed as Lady of the Bedchamber to Caroline, Princess of Wales (not a woman who was ever in Sarah's good books). She married the Earl of Montagu, and they had five children. She was the only Marlborough child to outlive her parents.

The Family of the 3rd Duke and Duchess

Charles Spencer became the 3rd Duke of Marlborough on the death of his aunt Henrietta, but, like his aunt, he could not get his hands on Blenheim while his grandmother was alive. It was stipulated in the terms of Marlborough's will that on inheriting the dukedom, the Spencer family estates at Althorp would revert to Charles's younger brother, John, thus ensuring the Spencer family would not end up bankrupted by Charles's extravagant spending. Charles would rent houses, spend vast sums on refurbishment, and when the owner terminated the lease or wanted the house back, he would rent another and spend yet another fortune on it. Deprived of Althorp and unable to move into Blenheim, Sarah intervened and installed Charles in the Royal Lodge at Windsor, a country house that was in her gift. But Charles continued to spend, making lavish alterations to the lodge and on top of that buying Monkey Island in the Thames to build a gilded banqueting pavilion and a fishing lodge. Money just poured through his hands and eventually relations

between Sarah and Charles hit an all-time low, and he left the lodge, borrowing huge sums to buy an estate at nearby Langley, which he rebuilt.

Desperate to keep the moneylenders at bay, Charles sued the Blenheim Trust for control of his inheritance. The court granted him a yearly pension of £5000 (almost a million in today's terms) but ruled that the entail remain intact. In spite of this favourable outcome, Sarah could foresee problems down the line, and she wisely restructured the trust so that each successive duke would only have a lifetime interest. An inventory was drawn up, separating Sarah's personal wealth and possessions from the entail. The problems were not over. Charles continued to live at Langley and to spend extravagantly. Sarah was rightly concerned that no money would be left to spend on Blenheim when the Palace would pass under Charles's control. She had every right to be worried. She hadn't lived there since the 1730s and the palace had deteriorated. This was Charles's view of the situation: "As for the question of my building at Blenheim, that depends upon her. If she will be so good as to die soon that I may be able to clear my debts, I believe I shall build, but if she is spiteful enough to live much longer, I fear I shall not build." Not surprisingly, Sarah cut Charles out of her will, leaving the bulk of her possessions and wealth to her favourite grandson, John (from whom the Earls of Spencer are descended).

The 3rd Duke did little to benefit Blenheim: his legacy amounts to this portrait (*left*), and a service of Meissen china exchanged with the king of Poland for a pack of staghounds. He did install elegantly carved bookcases in the Long Gallery to house the 24,000 volumes that constituted the Sunderland Library, "the finest library in Europe," collected by his father. The books were moved from Sunderland House in London to Blenheim in 1749. The books were sold, and the bookcases ripped out by the 7th Duke.

Sarah did not approve of her grandson's choice of bride, Elizabeth Trevor, who was the daughter of a political opponent. She wrote in a letter to a friend: "I think it a very improper match for a man that might have had anybody, without being at all in love with the person, to marry a woman who's [sic] father is a mighty ridiculous man, a family of beggars and all very odd people." And there's more, saying "she has very bad teeth, which I think is an objection alone in a wife, and they will be sure to grow worse with time."

DIANA, DUCHESS OF BEDFORD, SISTER OF THE 3RD DUKE

"Dear Little Di" as she was affectionately known by her family, was orphaned at the age of six when she joined the household of her grandmother Sarah. She was her grandmother's favourite and closest confidante, described as "having more sense than anybody I know of my sex." Sarah tried to arrange a secret marriage with Frederick, Prince of Wales, the unpleasant, estranged son of George II, but that scheme was frustrated by Prime Minister Robert Walpole. She married the handsome Lord John Russell, Duke of Bedford, who turned out to be a cold-hearted husband. She died far too young, at the age of twenty-five, after a stillbirth, a miscarriage and a bout of tuberculosis.

Charles, 3rd Duke of Marlborough

Elizabeth Trevor, 3rd Duchess of Marlborough

The 4th Duke and Duchess and his Sister

GEORGE, 4TH DUKE OF MARLBOROUGH

left George Spencer, the 4th Duke was only nineteen when he inherited the title and the estates. He was handsome and very rich but also intensely shy and sensitive. He was pursued relentlessly by the pushy mamas of every eligible young lady in the country. He enjoyed his brief bachelorhood until he was finally cornered by Lady Caroline Russell.

This was a golden age for Blenheim, with parties, hunts, games and eight children running around. It became a glamourous and elegant palace that delighted visitors and impressed royalty. The Duke indulged his passion for collecting carved gemstones, the famous Marlborough gems, and for astronomy. He built an observatory in the palace from where he would chart the movements of stars and planets. But his inherent shyness and chronic hypochondria eventually got the better of him and he retreated from the world and from his children. A contemporary wrote: "[The Duke] dreaded anything that could in any way ruffle the tranquil monotony of his existence … it is said that he remained for three years without pronouncing a single word." His eldest son and heir was a profligate spender and a great disappointment to his parents. His duchess died in 1811. After her death, he never left Blenheim or the grounds again until he died in his sleep in 1817.

CAROLINE, 4TH DUCHESS OF MARLBOROUGH

right The Duchess was not happy with her depiction in the family group painting, and another portrait of her alone was duly commissioned. Caroline Russell was not intimidated by inheriting Blenheim, as she had grown up at the almost equally grand Woburn Abbey. She embraced the task of rejuvenating the dark, old-fashioned furnishings and dreary damasks that had remained unchanged since Sarah's day with a cheerful palette of yellows, blues, and greens. On her deathbed, she reconciled with her son, whom she had not seen for eighteen years.

DIANA SPENCER, SISTER OF THE 4TH DUKE

Biographical notes describe her as "English Noblewoman and artist." A frequent visitor to Blenheim, the 4th Duke's sister, Lady Diana, was a lively, interesting and talented woman of great spirit. She had been married off to Lord Bolingbroke, an unpleasant, unfaithful bully of a man. She found solace in the arms of the impecunious Viscount Topham Beauclerk, described as "celebrated wit and friend to Dr. Johnson." Bolingbroke divorced Diana for adultery, which in those days was referred to as "criminal conversation." Within two days of the decree, Diana and Topham were married and soon produced four children. Topham later became ill and drug-addicted and died aged only forty. As is so often the case for women artists, it took her husband's death to kick-start her artistic flowering.

CAROLINE DUCHESS OF MARLBOROUGH 1779

The 5th Duke and Duchess

left George was "The Profligate Duke," as his biographer and descendant, Mary Soames, described him in the book of the same name. George ran wild, spending vast sums of money he did not have. In 1798 he purchased Whiteknights, near Reading, a grand house with a grand park, now part of Reading University. There he laid out extravagant gardens with the rarest of plants and held the wildest of parties and was subsequently declared bankrupt. It was not just plants that were his passion. Although he married Lady Susan Stewart, *right*, in 1791 and had four children with her, he managed a high-profile affair with Lady Mary Ann Stuart that culminated in court proceedings, and he then took as his mistress a local girl, Matilda Glover, with whom he fathered another four, maybe six, children. Matilda moved in and Susan moved out. He eked out an existence on a tiny pension, living off fish and game from the park and wine from the cellars – all funds had been depleted, all Blenheim treasures (luckily) entailed, apart from the wine. The diarist Harriet Arbuthnot visited in 1824: "The present Duke is overloaded with debt, is very little better than a common swindler and lets everything about Blenheim. People may shoot and fish at so much per hour and it has required all the authority of a court of Chancery to prevent his cutting down all the trees in the park."

One saving grace: It was the 5th Duke who reclaimed the Churchill name by royal licence. The family have been Spencer-Churchill ever since.

The 6th Duke and Duchess

right George Spencer-Churchill inherited a very run-down, shabby Blenheim; he did do something about it, however, raising money on mortgages to renovate and repair it. But he was a gambler who didn't always, by some accounts, pay his debts. He served as Lord Lieutenant of Oxfordshire and as the Tory MP for Chippenham and later for Woodstock, the family seat. He fathered about eight children, went through a fake marriage with a sixteen-year-old with whom he had a child, then legally married three of his cousins (one after the other, thankfully), and stipulated in his will that all his papers should be burned, leaving a gap in the archives and a lot of questions unanswered.

The 7th Duke and Duchess

JOHN, 7TH DUKE OF MARLBOROUGH

above The 7th Duke was a true Victorian, in the sense that he was driven by high-mindedness, duty, and God. He was a dutiful politician, serving in the Cabinet and as Lord Lieutenant of Ireland under Disraeli. As Tory MP for Woodstock he campaigned to strengthen the influence of the church by banning Sunday trading and forbidding bands from playing in parks on a Sunday in case it afforded amusement to the public. Where he inherited these traits from is hard to work out. It can't have been from his father or grandfather.

Blenheim took on the air of a gloomy, overstuffed Victorian parlour. Any guest wanting to admire the nine Titian paintings, *The Loves of the Gods*, given to the 1st Duke by the Duke of Savoy, would have been disappointed. The paintings were considered by the Duke too raunchy to remain on view and were banished to the kitchen wing from their prime position in the Great Hall along with *The Rape of Prosperine*, a priceless Rubens painting. There was never enough money for the upkeep of Blenheim or for funding the rackety

lives of the eight children he had with his solid, dutiful wife, Frances Vane. The solution was a word in the ear of the then Lord Chancellor, who pushed through an Act of Parliament undoing the entail that Sarah had so wisely set in place to protect Blenheim's treasures. He started by selling off the Sunderland Library (a contribution from the 3rd Duke) and the Marlborough gems (lovingly collected by the 4th Duke). The scandal surrounding his sons' behaviour in an attempt to blackmail the Prince of Wales over his misdeeds with married women led to his taking up the post of Lord Lieutenant of Ireland at a particularly tricky time. He acquitted himself well, but the stresses and strains of trying to keep up appearances led to a massive heart attack and he died aged sixty-one.

FRANCES, 7TH DUCHESS OF MARLBOROUGH

below Frances Vane, the 7th Duchess, who even in youth looked middle-aged. "A kind-hearted, motherly sort of person—neither clever nor at all handsome," as one visitor described her. She produced eleven children, eight of whom survived childhood. Blenheim was primarily a home for this brood. Their two sons (George the heir and Randolph the spare) gave their parents no end of trouble, reacting to their father's "overbearing manner and assumptions of superiority." Following the death of her husband, Frances took up good works and was proud of a letter from Queen Victoria commending her work for famine relief.

The 8th Duke, his Duchesses, his Brother, and his Brother's Wife

GEORGE, 8TH DUKE OF MARLBOROUGH

opposite It is hard to know where to begin with the amorous adventures of George Charles Spencer-Churchill. He fell briefly in love with Lady Albertha Hamilton, by all accounts a brainless beauty, married her but quickly tired of her. He had an affair with a married woman, Edith, Lady Aylesford, with whom he had an illegitimate child. A huge scandal ensued, made worse by an attempt by George's brother, Randolph, to force the Prince of Wales to intervene. The entire family was frozen out of society for years. George reconciled with Albertha for a while, but he failed to resist the temptation of the lovely Lady Colin Campbell and was cited in her divorce. Then he finally faced his own divorce from Albertha, who had had enough.

When George inherited the title, he had no wife, an expensive lifestyle and precious little money. He

continued to sell off Blenheim treasures released from entail thanks to his father's intervention. All the best paintings went, then all the porcelain and china. It was a devastation. George spent the money on his own passions: farm buildings, laboratories for his scientific experiments and hot houses for his exotic plants. During his sell-off frenzy he was introduced to Lilian Hammersley, a wealthy, attractive widow, and they married in New York in 1888. Her money was used to fix the roof, install electricity, central heating and a telephone system devised by the Duke, build a boathouse and buy an organ. He immersed himself in his science and his plants and all should have been well, but he was always restless and he died suddenly, aged forty-eight. Was he all bad? A contemporary commented that, "I had known [him] from a boy, a youth of great promise marred from fate, shining in many branches of human endeavour, clever, capable of great industry, and within measurable distance of reaching conspicuous success in science, mathematics and mechanics." Perhaps he had been marred by fate, the unforeseen result of a cold, puritanical upbringing?

ALBERTHA HAMILTON, HIS FIRST WIFE

left She was beautiful and innocent but dim, and given to childish practical pranks. Known as "Goosie," Albertha's mother-in-law remarked that she was "stupid, pious and dull." She and the 8th Duke had four children together during their unhappy marriage, and she sued for divorce just as George was to inherit the dukedom.

"B"

The Marquis of Blandford

LILIAN HAMMERSLEY, HIS SECOND WIFE

below From a well-to-do military family based in New York, Lilian Price first married the millionaire Louis Hammersley, who died in 1883, leaving her a rich young widow. Her second marriage to the dashing if seriously flawed George Spencer-Churchill, 8th Duke of Marlborough, took place in 1888 after a speedy courtship. She used her fortune to bring much needed renovations to Blenheim, but after her Duke died in 1892, she sued his heir for the return of her money. She married for a third time to Lord William de la Poer Beresford, and they had one child. She died in 1909, aged fifty-five, and is buried in the Beresford family crypt in Ireland.

RANDOLPH SPENCER-CHURCHILL, AND JENNIE JEROME, HIS BROTHER AND SISTER-IN-LAW

opposite Randolph was charismatic, charming, clever, a little cruel, and often badly behaved. However, he had more luck in love than his brother. Aged twenty-four, he met the beautiful Miss Jennie Jerome of New York on a Tuesday and by the Friday they had agreed to marry. She was a free-spirited American with a snake tattooed

on her wrist and, not surprisingly, his parents completely disapproved, deeming her parents vulgar. Eight months after they first met, Randolph and Jennie were married at the British Embassy in Paris. His parents did not attend the wedding. The newlyweds settled in Curzon Street, London, and lived in a whirl of "gaiety and excitement." They had two sons, Winston and Jack. Randolph looked to have a promising political career within the Tory party as Secretary of State for India and Chancellor of the Exchequer, but his controversial views and his lack of understanding of the political mood caused all that promise to fizzle out. His biographer wrote: "Churchill had eleven months in office and was without rival in attracting so much attention and achieving so little." But he was not well. He was treated for the symptoms of syphilis for over twenty years and died in 1895 at forty-five years of age.

Jennie's dashing, handsome and unreliable father, Leonard, was a New York stockbroker who made and lost millions and had affairs all over town. He was a template for most of the men in her life. As a teenager, Jennie lived with her mother and sisters in Paris, where she attracted a lot of attention. Her mother was hoping to marry her off to a prince, not the second son of a duke. After her marriage, Jennie spent much time at Blenheim and, as is well-known, it was there that she gave birth to her first child, Winston. The marriage was not going well, and there were tensions with her mother-in-law. Jennie looked after her two sons in a distant sort of way. She lived her own life, played the piano, wrote plays, and worked for the Red Cross. She had several lovers, including the Prince of Wales, but stood by Randolph as he sickened and died. She then married George Cornwallis West, a captain in the Scots Guards who was only days older than her son, but that only lasted a couple of years. Her third marriage was to Montagu Phippen Porch, who was younger even than Winston.

Jennie and Winston grew very close over his adult life, and Winston treated her as a confidante rather than a mother. When asked if he had liked his father, he replied: "How could I? I was ready enough as a boy, but he wouldn't let me. He treated me as if I had been a fool; barked at me whenever I questioned him. I owe everything to my mother; to my father, nothing." She died after surgery to treat a broken leg and is buried next to Randolph in the Marlborough family plot.

Portrait Album

G. PÉNABERT, Phot.   PASSAGE DU HÂVRE, 36 & 38

Charles Spencer-Churchill, Duke of Marlborough, Consuelo Duchess of Marlborough, John Marquess of Blandford, Lord Ivor Spencer-Churchill.

The Family of the 9th Duke

CHARLES, 9TH DUKE OF MARLBOROUGH

opposite The 8th Duke died unexpectedly leaving Charles, his twenty-year-old student son with the burden of Blenheim. Named "Sunny" because he was titled Earl of Sunderland, he wasn't at all sunny of disposition. He was a well-educated, intelligent, melancholic individual. As a young man he had a successful career in the army and subsequently in politics as a member of the House of Lords. He went on to become a Knight of the Order of the Garter, just like his illustrious ancestor the 1st Duke. He held many other significant posts, proving to be a well-respected member of the community. He was very close to his cousin, Winston Churchill, who understood him and the dilemma of his position. With his intelligence he could have probably enjoyed a successful career in business, but unfortunately that was not part of his birth status agenda.

Sunny soon realised that after so many generations of dukes had squandered the estate and sold off priceless artefacts and land, the only way for Blenheim to survive as a family home was for him to marry into wealth. Encouraged by his grandmother, Fanny, he sacrificed love and happiness and entered into a marriage with Consuelo Vanderbilt. He had a strong sense of duty and a love of Blenheim and everything aesthetic, thus he was well-placed to make significant changes. Fortunately, he spent Consuelo's large dowry well, employing French decorators to enhance the staterooms (with the help of his wife's exquisite taste and influences from her time spent in Paris) and most notably the creations of the Water Terraces and the Italian Gardens, assisted by Achille Duchêne. The marriage was doomed from the start, however, and Sunny and Consuelo separated and later divorced.

CONSUELO VANDERBILT, 9TH DUCHESS OF MARLBOROUGH

opposite and following page It is thanks to her loveless marriage to my great-grandfather Sunny that Blenheim is still in family hands today after nearly 320 years.

Consuelo's father, William Kissam Vanderbilt, a self-made railroad millionaire and her mother, Alva Erskine Smith, a southern belle from Mobile, Alabama, were ambitious and part of the prosperous Gilded Age. Living between New York and Newport, Rhode Island, Consuelo was accustomed to a lavish lifestyle and entertained on a grand scale; however, it was not part of her life plan to be forced into a loveless marriage far away from family and friends.

Alva had other ideas. She saw her daughter's marriage to a suitable English aristocrat as a stepping stone into snobbish established New York society. In 1895, Alva got her sobbing daughter, under duress, to the altar in New York. Sunny received Consuelo's considerable dowry of $2.5 million dollars (approximately $85 million today). With money in hand, Sunny started on the renovations to Blenheim immediately. He set about buying art as well as building a substantial London home, Sunderland House, in Mayfair.

On arriving in England Consuelo threw herself into the role of duchess with relative ease, the only hindrance being other female members of the Spencer-Churchill family who had little patience with the young American and disliked their roles being usurped. Consuelo, on the other hand, soon won the respect of servants, tenants and villagers and made it her life's work to look after those less fortunate. She was readily accepted into the London social scene. Men were captivated by her beauty and intelligence, and she thoroughly enjoyed the stimulating company and welcomed the escape from her husband's constant criticism and scrutiny at Blenheim.

As was expected, she duly produced two sons, my grandfather, Bert, born in 1897 and Ivor born in 1898. With duty done and plenty of money for the Duke to spend on restoration, Consuelo and Sunny spent less and less time together. Following affairs on both sides, they separated in 1906, although divorce was not granted until 1921 and the marriage was annulled in 1926. Divorce being socially unacceptable in aristocratic circles, the process took time.

Consuelo went on to have a happy second marriage with the successful entrepreneur and aircraft pioneer Jacques Balsan, and they lived and created homes in both France and America.

GLADYS DEACON

left and below left After the divorce, Sunny married another French-American socialite, the famously beautiful and fascinating Gladys Deacon (she pronounced it Glay-diss). She was a friend of both Consuelo and the Duke and was invited to spend weekends at Blenheim, where her relationship with Sunny began. Her troubled, unstable childhood led her to immersing herself in culture and art and developing an obsession with the English nobility and their estates. However, after successfully trapping Sunny into marriage, Gladys soon tired of the Duke and their mundane life at Blenheim. She had stopped socialising due to botched plastic surgery on her nose and jawline, and consoled herself with spaniels. And more spaniels. In the end she had about forty-five Blenheim spaniels messing priceless rugs and chewing on gilded chair legs. Evicted finally from Blenheim, she took her dogs with her. All that beauty, all that talent to amuse and she ended her life as a reclusive "crazy dog lady" in an isolated farmhouse in Oxfordshire, eventually dying in a mental hospital. She did, however, leave her mark: her notorious blue eyes were painted under the portico and her face is depicted on the sphinxes in the Water Terraces. Her legacy lives on.

WINSTON CHURCHILL

opposite Winston Churchill hardly needs an introduction. His ties to Blenheim went well beyond his being born there, however: he spent a lot of time there as child; proposed to his Clementine in the garden; and painted and wrote there, inspired by the beauty of the place and the tranquillity he found. He was close to his cousin, Sunny, and his first wife, Consuelo. After their divorce he spent many happy times with Consuelo and Jacques at their home in the South of France, a welcome respite from the cares of state.

The 10th Duke and Duchess

BERT, 10TH DUKE OF MARLBOROUGH

I think that my grandfather was somewhat lucky: he was of the generation where his life was already set out for him from birth, and his mother was very wealthy, which allowed him to enjoy a lavish, slightly self-indulgent lifestyle without too many responsibilities.

He followed the family tradition of being educated at Eton followed by a short stint at Sandhurst before serving in the Life Guards (a unit now part of The Household Cavalry) and fighting in the First World War. He married Mary Cadogan in 1920, and they went on to have five children, four of them between 1921 and 1929. Charles, my late uncle, was a very much welcome afterthought in 1940.

Their early life was spent at Lowesby Hall in Leicestershire while his father was still living at Blenheim. Here he was able to pursue no end of country pursuits: hunting, fishing, shooting, gardening, playing croquet and bridge, at all of which he was a master. He inherited in 1934 and moved into Blenheim. Mary was the perfect mother and hostess, and they entertained lavishly while at the same time ensuring their children had a disciplined, balanced and well-rounded family upbringing.

Bert was conscious of the lack of creature comforts at Blenheim and went about installing bathrooms—not an easy task in a building made of solid stone. In 1950, realising the need for additional income, he opened areas of the palace and grounds to the public and instigated a more business-like approach to keeping Blenheim sustainable for future generations. He was one of the originators of the "stately homes" model.

MARY CADOGAN, 10TH DUCHESS

It is very sad to note that my great-grandmother, Consuelo, and grandmother, Mary, died so soon after one another when I was young, so I have very little recollection of either, but hold them both in huge regard.

Mary was born a Cadogan, daughter of Viscount Chelsea, whose family owned swathes of London. Being a daughter, however, didn't secure you wealth, but Bert's parents were thrilled and relieved with his sensible choice. She dedicated her short life to ensuring Blenheim and the local community were seen to be working hand-in-hand, giving much of her time during the war to the Auxiliary Territorial Service and Red Cross, as well as serving as a local Justice of the Peace.

The 11th Duke and his Duchesses

JOHN GEORGE VANDERBILT HENRY,
11TH DUKE OF MARLBOROUGH, "SUNNY"

The 11th Duke was the second to have the nickname "Sunny" (derived from the courtesy title Earl of Sunderland). My father, however, enjoyed a much sunnier disposition than his grandfather.

My father followed an early career similar to that of his father—educated at Eton and serving for seven years in the Life Guards, part of that time posted to Germany when he was married to my mother, Susan Hornby. Their marriage in 1951 was a large society wedding at St Margaret's Westminster attended by many members of the Royal Family and aristocracy. It had the makings of a fairy-tale marriage: a dashing couple with a huge number of friends and a busy social life. Sadly, it didn't last. They had the added tragedy of losing my elder brother, John, at the age of nearly three, but they went on to have my brother, James, in 1955 (the current 12th Duke) and myself in 1958 before separating.

I have no recollection of my parents being together, and as a child I largely lived with my father, spending part of the holidays and some weekends with my mother. Luckily, I had the support of our loving nanny, Audrey Highmore, and it was she who provided much of the stability in my young life.

My father's second wife was Tina Livanos, who had previously been married to Aristotle Onassis. She had two children with him: Alexander and Christina, who became very much part of our life at Lee Place, our home at the time. The marriage lasted ten years and we were sad to see her go, having enjoyed a fun-packed life full of adventures in Greece and St. Moritz.

In 1972, my grandfather Bert died, but by this stage my father was already well-versed in the role of running Blenheim, so he stepped into it with relative ease. Soon after, he married Rosita Douglas and they had three children: Richard, who sadly died at a young age, and then in 1974 Edward and in 1977 Alexandra.

My father had a similar attitude to that of his namesake Sunny and understood that his life's work was to ensure that Blenheim could be handed over to the next generation in better condition than he found it. He witnessed a huge amount of change during his lifetime and largely embraced the change that saw Blenheim go from being a family home to becoming a huge and successful commercial enterprise.

The Family of the 12th Duke

CHARLES JAMES,
12TH DUKE OF MARLBOROUGH

My brother and I had a complicated upbringing. Being born into a family where your life from birth is already mapped out for you is not easy.

Our parents' generation was probably the last to be able to live in and maintain these grand stately homes with inherited wealth, but as their assets became depleted over many decades, our present generation is forced to be more commercial and innovative to keep the estates intact. The annual cost of maintaining Blenheim is immense, but we are fortunate to have opportunities to raise income through outside revenues received from visitors. We have a modern commercial infrastructure to manage day-to-day activities, and so the role of duke that my brother succeeded to is likened to a figurehead or a chairman who will ensure that with hard work now the estate will hopefully be left in a better state for the following generations.

James went to Harrow and then carried out a short stint in the army (as was expected from his generation, especially if university was not on the agenda). He loves the land and country pursuits. As children we spent a lot of time learning about the estate from our father, who had an equal passion for Blenheim. James is now a member of the Woodstock Town Council, a role he takes seriously as it allows him to see and hear the views from local constituencies and to see the other side of the coin. James is also passionate about trying to rebuild the art collection and replace or reacquire family paintings that had been sold off. Of course, with limited funds this is not always possible, but with help from our own foundations some exciting reacquisitions have come back home to the palace.

James's son, George, from his first marriage to Rebecca Few-Brown, will become the 13th Duke. He has two other children, Araminta (born 2007) and Caspar (born 2008) with his second wife, Edla Griffiths, whom he married in 2002.

GEORGE, MARQUIS OF BLANDFORD

When George eventually becomes the 13th Duke, he will hopefully be in the fortunate position of finding the estate and palace in much better shape both financially and structurally, having benefited from a long period of restoration work. Living in Blenheim as a family home is not so easy these days because of the endless annual events and lack of privacy; nonetheless, it is a wonderful place to entertain, and it is my hope that it will stay as a family home for many generations to come.

left My brother, James, and his wife, Edla, the 12th Duke and Duchess.

opposite My nephew, George, and wife, Camilla, with their daughter, Olympia.

CHAPTER TWO

THE ARCHITECTURE

THE ARCHITECTURE

The Battle of Blenheim, fought in and around the small Bavarian village on the banks of the river Danube on 13th August 1704, was a magnificent victory, an unexpected one in the ongoing wars of the Spanish succession that put France on the back foot and reflected gloriously on Britain. It was cleverly masterminded by my charismatic ancestor, Captain-General of the allied forces, John Churchill, 1st Duke of Marlborough.

A relieved nation and a grateful monarch cast about for a suitable, monumental, heroic thank you. For Queen Anne, besotted at the time by Sarah, John's captivating Duchess, only the grandest of palaces would suffice. The site chosen was the Royal Manor of Woodstock in Oxfordshire, a royal park and residence that had seen better days. The plan was more than ambitious—to conjure up something akin to Versailles. The choice of architect was left to the Duke and Duchess. The naturally frugal Sarah, who could foresee endless budget troubles looming over this grandiose plan, suggested the tried-and-tested Christopher Wren, but the Duke chose John Vanbrugh, convivial fellow member of the Kit-Kat club, soldier, spy, wine merchant, playwright, and latterly self-taught architect. What could possibly go wrong?

opposite Oil on canvas by John Wootton, c. 1743, depicting the Battle of Blenheim fought on August 13th, 1704. The original is in the National Army Museum.

following pages A spectacular aerial view of the palace. The landscape is looking rather parched after a hot, dry summer.

The Building of Blenheim

It started well. Plans were drawn. The foundation stone was laid on the 18th of June 1705, hardly a year after the famous victory. By this time there were more than 1,000 workmen swarming around the site. The old manor house had been demolished and cleared, the foundations dug, and the site prepared under the supervision of the royal gardener, Henry Wise. It was not to be an easy build. The flamboyant John Vanbrugh was intent on building, "more a Monument to the Queen's Glory than a private Habitation for the Duke." Sarah, whose aesthetic tended to the comfortable and plain, wanted a fitting home for her gallant Duke. The Duke was all for monumental, but his commitments on the battlefields of Europe took him away from home, and Queen Anne blew hot and cold with a budget (that had never been agreed upon) depending on how her relationship with Sarah was faring.

Vanbrugh's vision for this massive palace was inspired by the dramatic Baroque palaces of Europe and his first great architectural success, Castle Howard. His triumphant, theatrical concept was shared by his collaborator in both Castle Howard and Blenheim, Christopher Wren's star pupil Nicholas Hawksmoor. Luckily, Hawksmoor had a firm grasp of technicalities, unparalleled engineering skills and an eye for detail, making the creative duo greater than the sum of its parts. Hawksmoor was responsible for much of the detailed design, and Christopher Wren, as surveyor General of Royal Works, stayed on the sidelines handing out advice. But the vision for this monumental mass of a building set so well in the landscape was Vanbrugh's alone. This grand, sprawling theatrical set-piece with its fantastical roofscape was designed to be best appreciated from a distance. The internal dimensions, with solid, thick walls and soaring, high ceilings, were never intended to be domestic.

One of the original plans from our archives, dated 1713. It is interesting to compare these plans to the layout today and see what was and was not built.

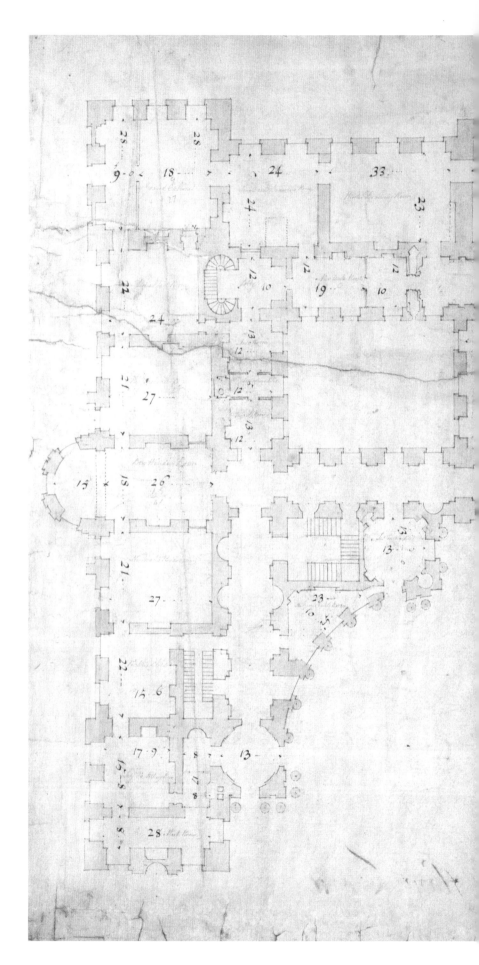

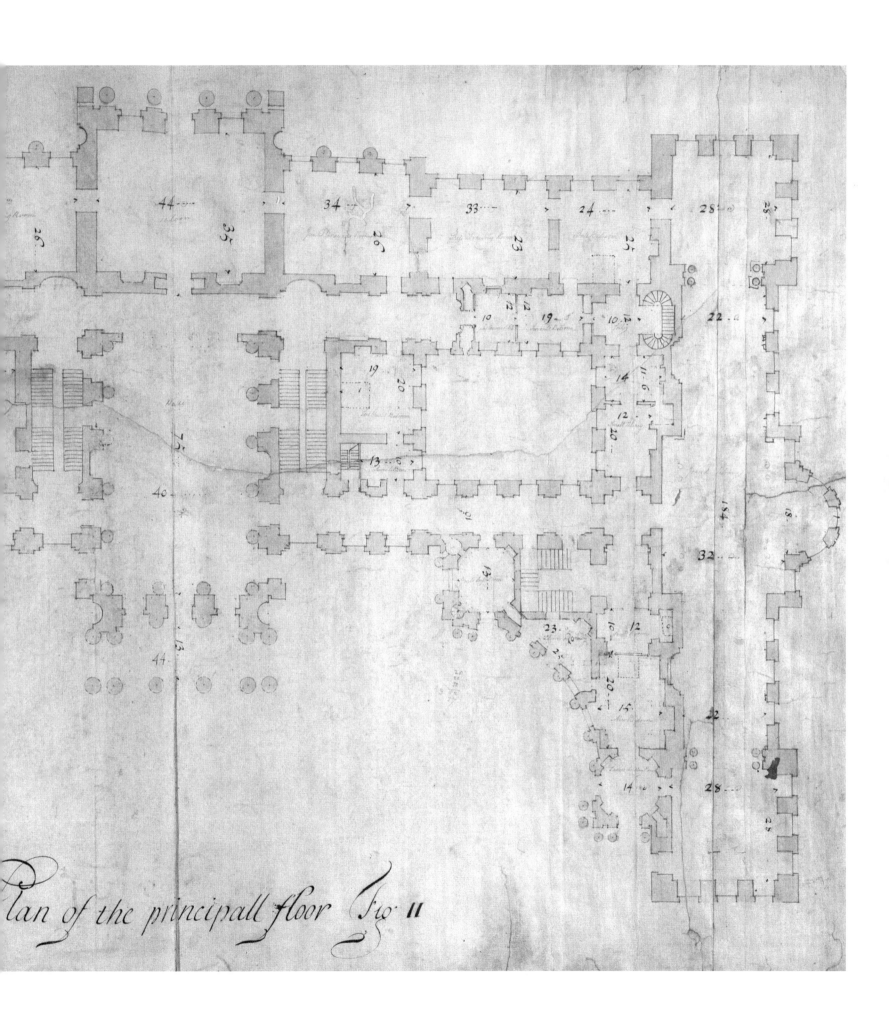

Plan of the principall floor Fig. II

previous pages A view from above showing the North Courtyard and details of one of the war trophy stone carvings by Grinling Gibbons located at the end of the East Colonnade.

above left Looking north over the clock tower between the Service Court and the Great Court. It shows the complexity of the roof structure, drains, and chimneys.

above right Beautiful autumnal evening light
emphasises the honey-coloured stone and
Capability Brown's lake, which transformed
the landscape back in the 1760s.

This grand, sprawling theatrical set-piece with its fantastical roofscape was designed to be best appreciated from a distance.

Moving In

The monumental scale of the Blenheim project meant it would take twenty-five years to build. The Churchill family continued to live at Holywell House in St. Albans, a large and comfortable manor house that had belonged to Sarah's family and which she inherited on her father's death. In 1709, already wearied by the battle of wills with Vanbrugh over Blenheim Palace, Sarah commissioned Christopher Wren to build Marlborough House in London. The Marlboroughs also had the use of Great Lodge in Windsor Park, which was part of the Crown Estate and close to their benefactor, Queen Anne. Sarah would have been quite happy to continue with these domestic arrangements, but the grand project of Blenheim appealed to her husband's sense of pride and achievement, and so Sarah set to with a will to make it happen. Marlborough was busy on the battlefields of Europe, but always on the lookout for artworks, gilded furniture and sumptuous fabrics to adorn his splendid Blenheim dream. He was shipping back velvets and damasks, paintings by Titian, Rubens, and Raphael and priceless collections of coins, medals, and statuary. A treasure trove was being amassed, with no walls (or ceilings), as yet, to contain them.

The major build took place between 1705 and 1712, providing well-paid jobs for the local population. There were serious problems with sourcing enough stone, as the local quarries were soon exhausted and a massive logistical operation was required to supply stone by horse and cart from more than twenty quarries as far afield as Plymouth and Portland, along with timber transported from the royal forests.

The plan was to landscape and build the park and gardens along with the palace, and to complete the East Wing, the private side of the palace, as a priority. But this grand project was beset by more problems than local shortages of stone and timber. Queen Anne had never specified who was going to pay for this monument: was it the Crown or the treasury or the Duke? Costs kept spiralling, and then disaster struck

in 1712. With Blenheim unfinished and uninhabitable, Queen Anne fell out irrevocably with her troublesome former lover Sarah. And her quarrels with both John and Sarah's politics escalated to such a degree that the pair went into voluntary exile in Europe to escape the wrath of their monarch.

The Duke was still an important figure in court circles, where he had many supporters, and by the summer of 1714 his tactical political deals and military successes were beginning to soften Queen Anne's stony heart. The Marlboroughs returned from exile on August 1st, only to discover, as they disembarked on English soil, that Queen Anne had died. Work on the still uninhabitable Blenheim, which had stopped in 1712, was resumed in 1716 under the new Hanoverian king, George I. But nothing was to run smoothly. Incensed by Sarah's meddling and demands, Vanbrugh left the project. Hawksmoor picked up the reins, but unpaid bills were piling up and no one was taking responsibility. Writs flew, and finally the Marlboroughs decided to finish Blenheim at their own expense. By 1719 the East Wing at least was habitable, and John and Sarah moved in. By this time, they were grandparents and all but two of their five children had died. John's health was not good, and he only had two summers left to him to enjoy his hard-won, monumental home.

opposite The North Courtyard portico with Corinthian columns supporting a pediment with a carved tympanum enriched with Grinling Gibbons carvings of the Marlborough coat of arms. It makes for an impressive main entrance.

The east façade, *above*, overlooking the Italian Gardens, with clipped hedges of yew and box as it is today, and, *below*, as it was in the nineteenth century before the 9th Duke's transformation.

opposite The south facade has a grand portico similar to that of the north, except the fluted Corinthian columns and pediment are less grand.

Voltaire wrote of Blenheim "If only the apartments were as large as the walls are thick, this mansion would be convenient enough".

After the Duke's death in 1722, Sarah renewed her efforts to finish the palace according to Vanbrugh's original vision, but she was never happy living there and used it only occasionally. Her last recorded visit was in 1735. She preferred to spend her old age in the more comfortable and familiar surroundings of Royal Lodge at Windsor and Marlborough House in London. But Blenheim was always on her mind. Sarah was a very astute businesswoman, and unlike most 18th-century women she enjoyed control over her finances throughout her marriage and widowhood, and she amassed a fortune. At one stage she was considered the richest woman in Britain. Being Sarah, she did meddle in her daughters' affairs, ensuring they made "good" marriages to ensure the Marlborough's standing at court and Blenheim's financial stability going forwards. These marriages may have seemed like a good idea at the time but did not result in winning at the game of Happy Families. Henrietta strayed and had a daughter by the playwright Congreve; Anne's husband, Charles Spencer, Earl of Sunderland, accused Sarah and John of treason, which was difficult to ignore. Sarah hated him. In her little private notebook, she damns his character and adds a physical description: "He had a very bad countenance, something very harsh in his face, white eyebrows eyelashes and eyes. He was late of a large make but had no more gentlenefs than a porter."

The dukedom passed (by special decree) to Henrietta, Sarah, and John's eldest surviving child. Sarah had fallen out with her eldest daughter because of her association with the London playwriting set that, of course, included her arch-enemy Vanbrugh. By all accounts Henrietta barely spent any time at Blenheim, and when she died at 52 in 1733, her spendthrift nephew, Charles Spencer, son of daughter Anne and the hated Sunderland, became the 3rd Duke of Marlborough. Sarah, who had often stepped in with grandmotherly concern during his harsh and neglectful upbringing, never thought much of his morals or his character, and he wisely waited until his formidable grandmother's death in 1744 to set about spending his inheritance.

In her gossipy notebook, Sarah describes her grandson in the ways he differs from his father, not necessarily in a good way:

He has much the advantage of him in his figure, he has a very good Person, and his face not ill, tho' there is something that resembles the Father's countenance, but a much softer look. The worst thing in his face is his Eyes, which are disagreeable, and have an unmeaning look; he has a very ill voice, speaks very little in Company, but if any body happens to contradict him, he will fall into a Pafsion, and answer as Brutally as his Father did & much more simply. But as Nobles go, as he is Duke of Marlborough, with a very great Estate, if he had been in good Hands, he would not have made an ill Figure in the House of Lords on the Duke's bench.

opposite The Great Hall looking south towards the Saloon and parkland towards Bladon. The imposing grand stone arch is supported by fluted columns with Corinthian capitals executed by Grinling Gibbons and his assistants. The keystone depicts Queen Anne's coat of arms.

The Architects

SIR JOHN VANBRUGH, 1664–1726

opposite Charming, brilliant, and well-connected, Vanbrugh was gifted with an extraordinary imagination and an ability to visualise in three dimensions. His early career experiences ranged from successful playwright to less-than-successful spy to desk-bound soldier. But it was as a self-taught architect that Vanbrugh's talents really shone. However, the architect and this particular client never saw eye to eye over the design or the cost, and Vanbrugh left the project in 1716 in a flurry of writs, court orders, and unpaid bills. After Blenheim, he completed several more grand and massive houses, slightly more restrained and subtle than Blenheim. But in Blenheim he had carried out the original brief from his monarch to build a monument to celebrate a martial triumph.

NICHOLAS HAWKSMOOR 1661–1736

right Taken on as a clerk by Sir Christopher Wren when he was only eighteen, Hawksmoor worked with Wren on grand projects such as Chelsea Hospital, St. Paul's Cathedral and Hampton Court Palace. With this solid grounding he emerged as a major architectural figure of the time. He collaborated with Vanbrugh on Blenheim Palace and took charge of the project after the acrimonious break between Vanbrugh and Duchess Sarah. Working on his own after Blenheim, Hawksmoor is best remembered for six of London's most beautiful churches.

ACCOLADES

Vanbrugh… was truly an artist: and prompted by the inspiration of genius he boldly dared to design an architectural picture. His subject was military and heroic: to commemorate a great battle and a great conquest, and to confer honour on its valiant commander. It was also to be a national palace, and demonstrative of a nation's wealth and liberality. With these considerations in view, he gave latitude to his pencil: he sketched freely, boldly, and vividly, confident that picturesque and interesting variety, and even beauty, might be thereby produced. In spite of the splenetic and illiberal strictures of Walpole, who calls it "a quarry of stone," he succeeded in designing and erecting an edifice of singular grandeur, elegance,

and appropriateness. "The most poetical of our architects," observes Mr. Soane in his fifth Lecture, "is Sir John Vanbrugh, whose palace at Blenheim confirms his power, and shows an extent of picturesque effect, variety of form, and contrast of masses, which delight the eye, and astonish the beholder. Indeed this work alone may be said to stamp him the Shakespeare of architects.

From A *Series of Picturesque Views of Noblemen's and Gentlemen's Seats, with Historical & Descriptive Accounts of each subject*, R. Havell & Son, 1823

To speak of Vanbrugh in the language of a painter, he had originality of invention, he understood light and shadow, and had great skill in composition. To support his principal object he produced his second and third groupes, or masses. He perfectly understood in his art what is the most difficult in ours, the conduct of the background, by which the design and invention are set off to the best advantage. What the back-ground is in painting, in architecture is the real ground on which the building is erected: and no architect took greater care than he that his work should not appear crude or hard ; that is, that it did not abruptly start ot of the ground without expectation or preparation.

Sir Joshua Reynolds, 1723–1792,
English painter

Not everyone was happy to see this vast palace built in the pleasant parklands of Woodstock. This acerbic caption to a contemporary engraving of Blenheim Palace draws attention to its extravagance and cost.

This Palace was erected at the Publick expence, in commemoration of the Battle of Blenheim and settled on the great Duke of Marlborough and his Descendants for ever. It stands upon a most delicious Spot of Ground in the large park of Woodstock: the ascent to it is through a long and Grand Avenue, over a Bridge of one Arch which cost above 20 000 £ building: From hence you enter a Great Gate under a handsome Tower into an open Court, on the sides of which are the Offices and Piazza's. The Offices are fit for 300 in family, and the out houses for the lodging a Regiment of Guards. The Palace is very noble both without and within, and extremely well adorned with Pillars, Pillasters, Collonades, Statues &c. The Garden is laid out in a magnificent manner and contains near -100 acres of ground. It requires the Royalty of a Sovereign Prince to support an Equipage suitable to the Greatnefs of this Palace.

Dear Mr. Bobart

Sarah wrote many, many letters to everyone involved in the build. Her secretaries copied these letters and many of the originals are now in the safe hands of the Bodleian Library in Oxford and the London Library.

Sarah had strong opinions about the build. She did want things to be perfect, but perfect in her way without wastage of time, money or materials, overwrought design and unnecessary elaborateness. She was on top of every detail. In many ways, she was the worst possible client an architect or interior designer could have.

The build started to go wrong when the local quarry ran out of stone and different stones were brought in. Sarah got totally involved in the placement of each stone. She wrote constantly to the Clerk of Works, Tilleman Bobart: (Edward Strong and Henry Banks were the principal masons for the early building works.) Here she's referring to the building shown on the following pages.

When I writ to you last, I thought the stone of the house and the stone of the office belongs to the same person, and might without prejudice to any body be employed where it was most pressing. But … upon examination I find the stone comes from two Different Quarrys and is worked by two severall men, the house by Mr. Strong and the offices by Mr. Banks and therefore to make Mr Banks amends and to employ his workmen I desire they may be set immediately to make the Garden wall, and that Mr Strong employs all his stone and men to finish that part of the house I have already recommended. By this means all the Business my Lord Marlborough would have done may go on with speed and all those things which are only Show may be left alone. I have ordered Mr Vanbrugh to proceed in this manner.

Sarah was not keen on unnecessary elaboration and was adamant about her priorities.

I suppose the Iron worke you mention in the Stair-cases in the clock tower which is already in hand, is quite plaine except that little part of which I took notice of when I was there, what is done of that sort can't be

left The "plaine iron worke" on the balustrade requested by Sarah.

opposite A letter from Sarah, copied by a secretary with a flourishing hand.

Mr: Bobart.

I am told that it is Probible the Building at Blenheim may be Delay'd for want of great Stone that lyes three or four miles further then the rest of the Quarrys, which by reason of the bad ways may not be brought in time, without an advance for the Carriage of it, of a halfpenny a foot, which will not come to above 40 or 50 Pound for this Summer, and for so small a Sum as that, one should be Sorry to have a great disappointment in a Building of so much Consequence to L:d Marlborough, therefore Pray Speak to M:r Joyne, in this matter, and do what is necessary to get the Stone In, in time, but take Care the you do it so, as that it may not remaine a president for the future—

I am yo:r Friend & Servant.

S: Marlborough

July the 26:th 1709.

To Mr: Bobart in Woodstock Parke

This is a true Copy

Jacob Wells

Thomas Gray.

A View of the Bridge.

Blenheim House

This Palace was erected at the Publick expence, in commemoration of
of Marlborough and his Descendants for ever. It stands upon a most deli
the ascent to it is through a long and Grand Avenue, over a Bridge
from hence you enter a Great Gate under a handsome Tower into an
and Piazza's. The Offices are fit for 300 in family, and the out hou
Palace is very noble both without and within, and extreamly well ado
The Garden is laid out in a magnificent manner and contains near
a Sovereign Prince to support an Equipage suitable to the Greatne

The East Front.

Battle of Blenheim and settled on the Great Duke
Spot of Ground in the large Park of Woodstock:
e Arch which cost above 20 000 £ building :
n Court, on the sides of which are the Offices
for the lodging a Regiment of Guards. The
with Pillars, Pilasters, Collars, Statues &c.
acres of Ground. It requires the Royalty of
of this Palace.

left An original engraving from the Bodleian Library showing the south façade with an interesting description of the house and comments on the cost and grandeur of the building. The upper left inset shows an image of Vanbrugh's bridge with the towers and colonnades that were never built.

overleaf A corridor on the north private side running from east to west is a series of stone arches supported on stone pilasters. Each section is topped with a mini-dome. If the wall at the end of the corridor was removed you would see all the way into the bow window of the Long Library.

Sarah was on top of every detail. In many ways, she was the worst possible client an architect or interior designer could have.

helped. *I wish to have no new worke begun without seeing a patterne, nor no more in the office wing of Iron worke that is not quite plaine except what is so far done that it cannot be helped … my meaning was as to the new offices, being perfectly useless … should goe no more Stone, money or hands to that worke that could possibly be employed in the carrying out of that part of the house my Lord Marlborough desires to be first finished.*

Sarah's priority was to finish the East Wing so they could move in

I have examined the directions the Duke of Marlborough left at his going away and find them to be as follows.

That the first worke to be finished is the Hall and Saloon. To compleat the steps up to the N portico being in number fourteen: To pave the hall and corridors with Portland and Black marble, the attick of the hall above the cornice on the inside to be covrerd with brick and finished for painting. The ceiling to be made plain without fretwork. The stair case on each side to be completed. And what they call the maine body of the house covered if possible. No iron work bspoke until I have seen the patterne. The bow window room all boarded plaine without parqueting Nothing to be done in the New Offices till all those things about the house which are more necessary are finished

Then, of course there were the money problems and politics to think about:

Mr. Joynes has been writ to by my order to send a very particular account of all that is due to every body by name, and for what you can do to prevent any disorder in the Election at Woodstock … it would be very uneasy for him (Marlborough) if there should be any Dispute … I charge you to forbid all works and expense and don't rely upon Mr. Vanbrugh of his doing of it. This paper shall be your warrant for it. Sept 28th 1710.

Inevitably, things were heating up between what Sarah wanted and what Mr. Vanbrugh wanted:

I have received your letter and give you many thanks for the account you gave me tho I did intend never to give any directions about the Buildings, I wonder much att Mr. Vanbrugh for what you write of his Orders. I always thought him a bold man but I think there are more that will worke upon the house unless he would give them better assurance than I fear he can of ever being paid. However I desire you will continue to let me know of all the mad things that are ordered.

By the end, there were unpaid bills, writs and court cases, and in 1721 the Marlboroughs unsuccessfully sued Vanbrugh, Hawksmoor and 419 other defendants for conspiracy. They were living in the East Wing at the time, surrounded by unfinished work. The Duke, who was not at all well, just wanted to find one part of the palace that was quiet. Vanbrugh fought back and flounced off the project:

These papers, madam, are so full of far-fetched laboured accusations, mistaken facts, wrong inferences, groundless jealousies, and strained constructions, that I should put a very great affront upon your understanding if I supposed it possible you could mean anything in earnest by them, but to put a stop to my troubling you anymore. You have your end, madam, for I will never trouble you more, unless the Duke of Marlborough recovers so far to shelter me from such intolerable treatment.

It is interesting to note that once the Duke had died, Sarah took on the financial burden of finishing Blenheim herself, recalling Hawksmoor and working more or less to Vanbrugh's plans – although she concentrated on reminders of her Duke's legacy, the Triumphal Arch and the Column of Victory, at the expense of finishing the stable court. She did pay Vanbrugh the outstanding £2,000 he was owed (well over half a million pounds today), but in a desire to keep the upper hand, she barred Vanbrugh and his wife from ever visiting the palace he had built. They had to be content walking around the grounds, which had always been open to the public.

above The entrance, known as the
Triumphal Arch, from the town of
Woodstock, designed by Hawksmoor
after the 1st Duke's death. It is of the
Corinthian order, and the flanking walls
of rusticated stone contain doorways with
large keystones carved with grotesque
masks of lions.

opposite The Column of Victory
commissioned by Sarah as a tribute
to her late husband, stands 134 feet
tall (forty-one metres). The Doric
column is topped with a statue of the
Duke dressed as a Roman general. The
inset engraving by Hawksmoor was a
suggestion for the design that obviously
influenced the finished column designed
by Lord Herbert.

Colonna Trajana d'Roma.

Who Lived Where

As is the custom with grand Baroque houses, the principal floor, or piano nobile, is on the entry level. In the case of Blenheim, the visitor's first impression is the breathtaking Great Hall that more than lives up to its name with a glorious, decorated ceiling sixty-seven feet (20.5 metres) high. Beyond the Great Hall, on the same central axis, is the impressive Saloon, with its trompe-l'oeil ceiling and minstrels' gallery overlooking the gardens to the south. Together, these two great rooms form the heart of the palace. Flanking the Saloon are two matching sets of state apartments for the grandest of visitors, each comprising an antechamber, a drawing room, and a bedchamber.

The 1st Duke and Duchess occupied the East Wing. Starting from the south-east corner was the Duke's study, or cabinet, followed by his antechamber and his bedchamber. The meeting place between the Duke's suite and the Duchess's was the Bow Window Room, a lovely, elegant, light-filled drawing room that was Sarah's favourite place to be. Sarah's apartment mirrored the Duke's, with a bedchamber and a dressing room. Each of the principal apartments was connected by hidden staircases to rooms for personal servants on the mezzanine floor above.

The Saloon would only have been used for dining on very grand occasions. The main family dining room was off the Great Hall on the east side, flanking one of the strategically and symmetrically placed light wells.

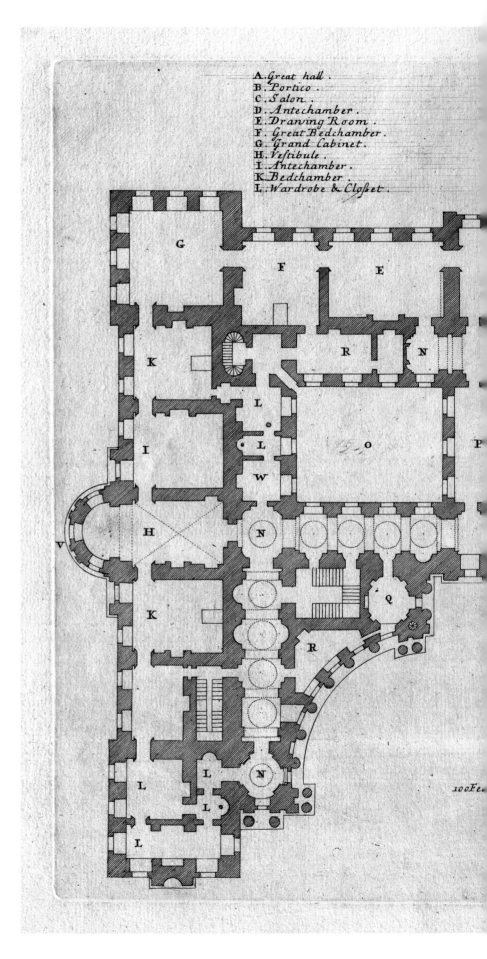

A. Great hall.
B. Portico.
C. Salon.
D. Antechamber.
E. Drawing Room.
F. Great Bedchamber.
G. Grand Cabinet.
H. Vestibule.
I. Antechamber.
K. Bedchamber.
L. Wardrobe & Closet.

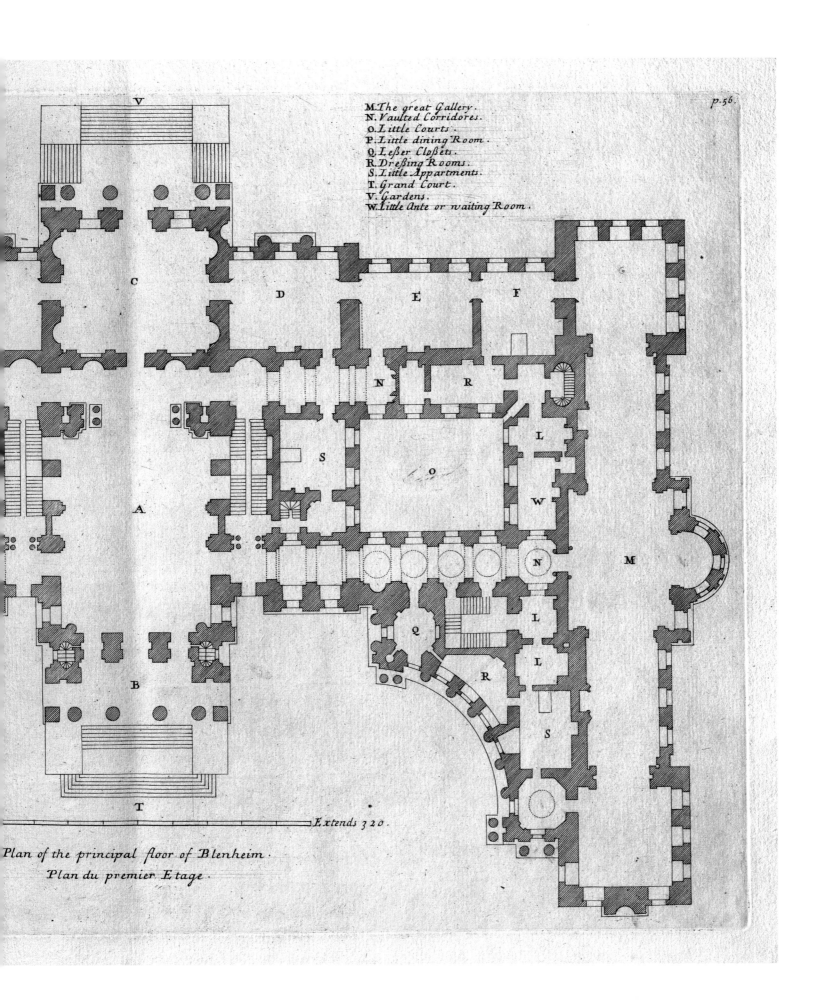

M. The great Gallery.
N. Vaulted Corridores.
O. Little Courts.
P. Little dining Room.
Q. Lesser Closets.
R. Dressing Rooms.
S. Little Appartments.
T. Grand Court.
V. Gardens.
W. Little Ante or waiting Room.

Extends 320.

Plan of the principal floor of Blenheim.
Plan du premier Etage.

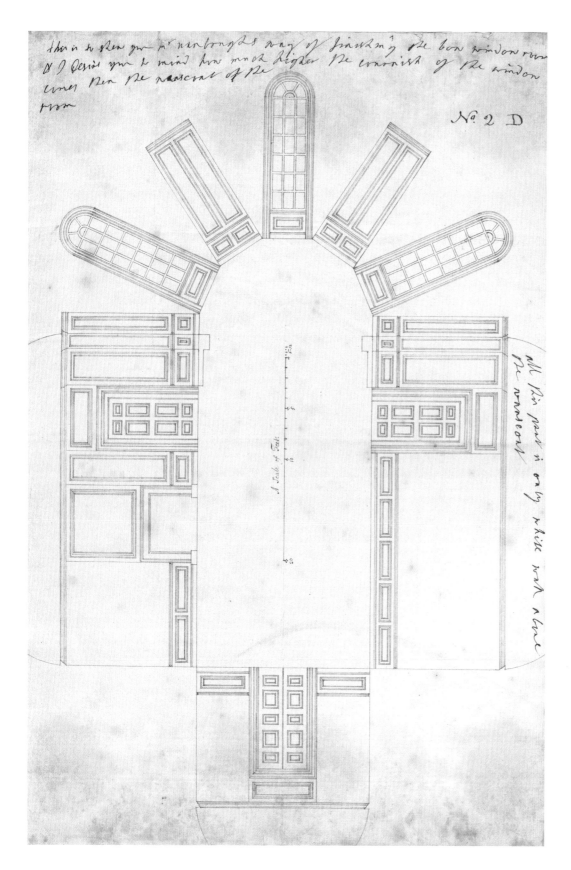

An original drawing by Hawksmoor for
the Bow Window Room, now used as our
private dining room.

The Bow Window Room today, with
the panelling and glazing very much as
imagined in Hawksmoor's drawing.

The south-west corner and the whole of the west side is occupied by the Great Gallery, designed by Nicholas Hawksmoor to house the Duke's impressive collection of art and artefacts from all over Europe. It vies for position as the longest room in Britain at 182 feet (fifty-six metres). Mirroring the family dining room and its dependencies on the east side are two apartments on the west side, one intended for Dean Jones, the Duke's chaplain (whom Sarah hated but tolerated because he played a mean hand of cards), and the other for Francis Godolphin, who was married to their daughter and heir, Henrietta (who was living in Bath at the time with her lover).

The principal rooms are linked by an enfilade, so the doors, aligned on a single axis, provide a vista through to successive rooms, making a grand processional route through the house. A long east-west vaulted corridor with saucer domes links the hall with the wings of the main block providing a 315-foot (ninety-six metres)

view from the bow window to the east to the bow window to the west. There are grand enough staircases, tucked behind the arcades, but there is no one sweeping statement staircase at Blenheim. As in the Baroque tradition, all the principal rooms are on the raised ground floor and there would have been no reason for worthy guests to bestir themselves from the piano nobile.

On the upper floor, interconnecting bedrooms and dressing rooms (no bathrooms, of course) were arranged into suites for family and friends. Sarah and John's granddaughter, Lady Anne Spencer, had an apartment with room for a female servant. Lady Pembroke, a fellow court official, serving as lady of the bedchamber to Princess Caroline, also had a suite of rooms. The attics, or garrets, and the rabbit warren of rooms on the mezzanine between the first and second floors were living quarters for servants accessed by narrow hidden staircases.

left The Long Library, which was modelled on designs by Hawksmoor, was originally planned as a picture gallery, but was furnished as a library from the time of the 3rd Duke onwards. The three ceiling panels were supposed to have murals by Sir James Thornhill, no doubt cancelled due to financial constraints.

opposite An enfilade of the three main state rooms from west to east. Blenheim was designed very symmetrically on all axes. The red carpet protects the parquet floors and defines the visitor tour route.

The basement mirrors the floor above, including the light wells. On the south side, rooms at garden level are accessed by the East Wing staircase, originally for family use; the vaulted rooms underneath the Great Gallery were intended for a grotto that was never built.

There was no kitchen in the basement because there was an entire Kitchen Court building to the east of the Great Court, mirrored (symmetry being the order of the day) by the stable block and chapel to the east. These massive service blocks were part of the grand plan, designed to add prestige and splendour to the aspect of the main building. Above the elaborate entrance gates to both, and disguised as heroic towers, were lead-lined water cisterns, providing a gravity-fed water supply. Windows on all sides of both outer courts were placed high up so the servants could not look out at the comings and goings of the family and guests, who were in turn spared the sight of the staff at work.

The kitchen block, built around the kitchen court, had a greenhouse and the kitchen on the south side, a bakehouse and a laundry either side of the entrance gate to the east and preparation spaces, drying rooms, and a servants' hall on the north side. Upper servants had their living quarters on the floor above.

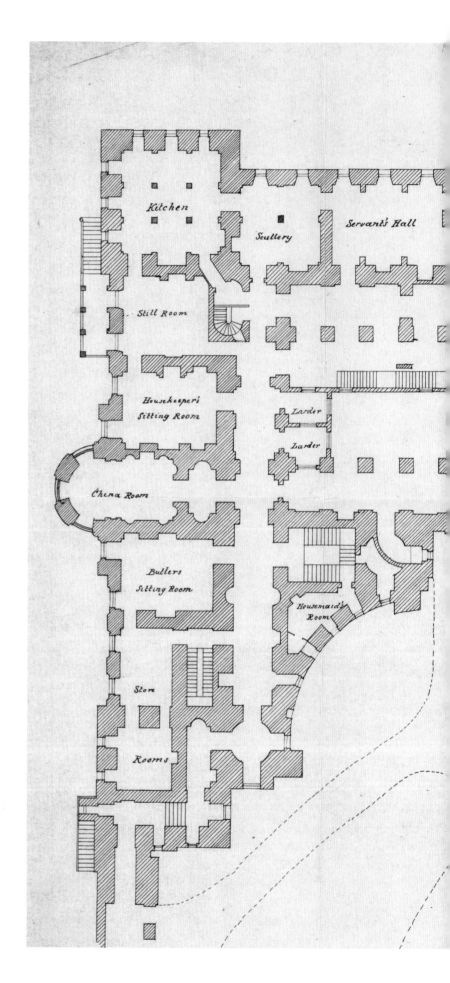

The lower ground floor as it was in the nineteenth century. Layouts today have changed but it is still used mainly as utility and service areas.

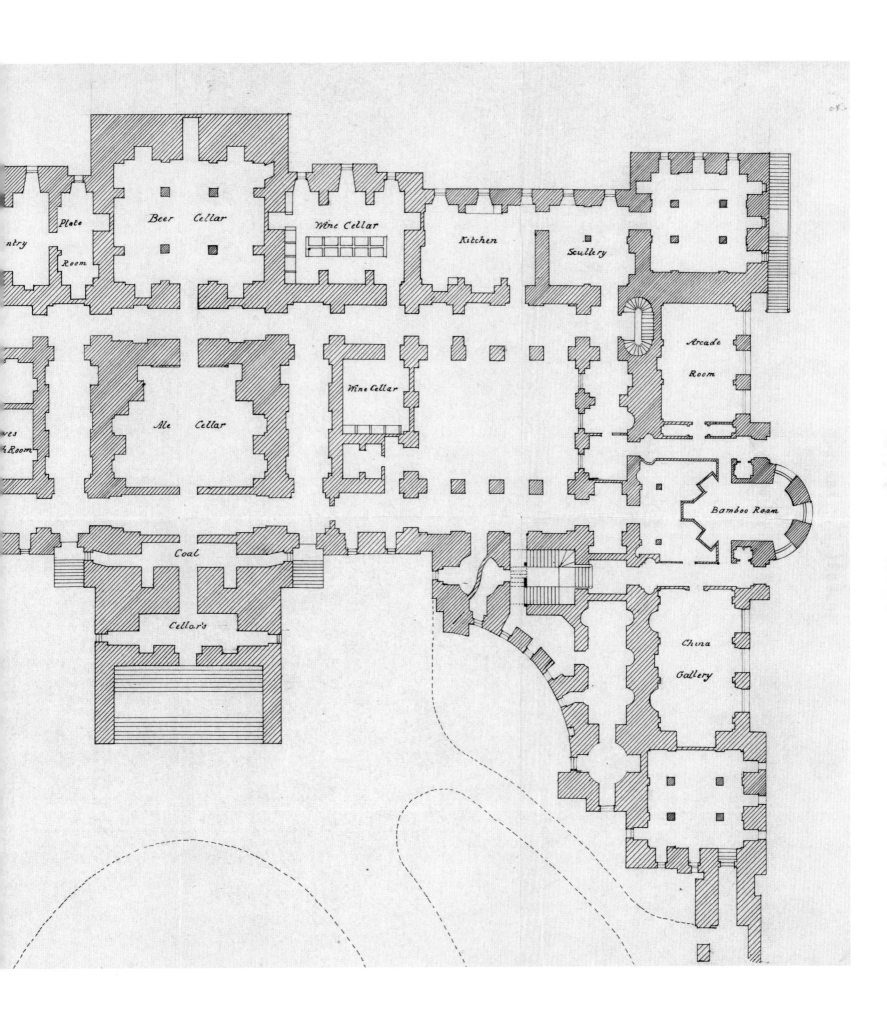

Plate

Room

Beer Cellar

Wine Cellar

Kitchen

Scullery

Arcade

Room

Ale Cellar

Wine Cellar

Bamboo Room

Coal

Cellar's

China

Gallery

The Chapel

Vanbrugh's original plans for the chapel were not realised by the time he walked off the project. Hawksmoor took over, and his hand in the final design is evident from the style of the pilasters and plasterwork, which are similar to his Great Gallery. But Sarah stepped in with objections to the interior elaborations and claimed the "very plain" finish proudly as her own, its plainness contrasting markedly with the rest of the house.

The Chapel was built after the 1st Duke's death under the Duchess's direction to designs by William Kent. This image shows it as it was as far back as I can remember: cold and draughty with yellow walls, very poor lighting and insulation. Fortunately it has been extensively renovated thanks to the generosity of our American foundation, and the colours of the eighteenth century have been restored.

Refurbishments and Improvements

Nothing much changed at Blenheim in the first half of the eighteenth century. The 3rd Duke commissioned carved bookcases to turn the Great Gallery into the Great Library for his father's collection of books. Unfortunately, the bookcases blocking windows to the north and south suffered from damp, while books on the east wall were exposed to sunlight, but it took a while for these problems to emerge.

With the succession of the 4th Duke, Blenheim blossomed. Much decorating was done, much art was acquired, lumpen dark furniture was consigned to the attics and the palace became a showcase for the best of British craftsmanship. The chapel was decorated, there were parties and dances and theatricals in the dramatically converted kitchen court Orangery. The suites of state bedrooms and antechambers along the south side were transformed into drawing rooms to display newly acquired picture collections, and 1st Duchess Sarah's favourite Bow Window Room became a billiard room. Carved-stone chimneypieces were inserted into rooms on the east and south fronts, and the Duke, keen scientist and astronomer that he was, set up a state-of-the-art observatory in the south-east tower. At this time, much of the basement was put to good use as wine cellars and storage, and dining halls for servants of every rank. In the park, Lancelot "Capability" Brown relandscaped Henry Wise's old-fashioned formal gardens, tore up the terracing of the Great Court and grassed it over, and created a magnificent lake, finally making sense of Vanbrugh's famous bridge.

The 5th Duke was a handsome, profligate rogue who spent his inheritance on exotic plants and racketing around with the Prince Regent. He didn't leave much of a mark on Blenheim other than rearranging the art, building a melon house in the Stable court, and creating some wildly decorated party rooms in the basement under the long library, the space originally earmarked by Vanburgh for a grotto.

opposite The built-in bookcases in the Long Library were installed by the 3rd Duke to house his vast collection of books, many of which he had inherited on the death of his older brother, Robert.

above A volume from our archives listing some of the volumes originally housed in the Library.

Each built-in bookcase was exquisitely designed to look like a freestanding piece of furniture. Surprisingly, there is no glass behind the grill doors, so keeping the volumes clean and dust free is an annual job.

The 6th Duke inherited a run-down, neglected building and no money in the bank. He borrowed extensively, raised mortgages and sold off timber. He spent a lot and not always wisely. He commissioned a lot of re-decorating and changed the use of public rooms. Moving with the times, the theatre/orangery became the Duke's offices, and the former kitchen was given over to the accounts department. In the dairy, butter and milk were cooled in an artificial stone fountain. New kitchens were created in the basement and a staircase built in the eastern light well to provide direct access to the dining room above. Blenheim acquired its own gasworks to service an underfloor heating system for the main corridors and a network of gaslight chandeliers. No more candles.

above The 5th Duke was an avid botanist and traveller who collected rare species. In the early nineteenth century he created this Indian Room in the undercroft with an exotic French panoramic mural. The room overlooked the west side before the water terraces were created.

opposite and right Gasolier light fittings installed by the 6th Duke. They have since been electrified, and the simple design fits seamlessly with any period.

The Seventh Duke brought his Victorian prudery to bear on Blenheim and all the airy, silken Georgian elegance (although tattered and torn) was buried under Victorian knick-knackery, fringed damask and screens.

Black-and-white photographs reveal how the rooms were decorated during the Victorian era and earlier.

opposite and top left The Long Library.

bottom left The Bow Window Room, now the dining room, as a cosy sitting room with a painted ceiling.
top right The main bedroom.
bottom right The Duchess's sitting room.

The 7th Duke brought his Victorian prudery to bear on Blenheim; all the airy, silken Georgian elegance (although tattered and torn) was buried under Victorian knick-knacks, fringed damask and screens. He went further than his father, contriving an Act of Parliament to break the entail to enable him to sell off Blenheim's treasures. He sold off the Sunderland Library, many paintings and countless invaluable objects. Alterations were made to the principal staircases, and the 5th Duke's melon house was removed. Under the 7th Duke's stewardship many of the rooms underwent yet another change of use, probably to accommodate his large family. (Over the years, so many different rooms have been designated State Bedroom and Billiard Room that it is hard to keep up.)

The 8th Duke continued enthusiastically selling off Blenheim's treasures. His passion (apart from women) was for science and botany. Profits from the sales went mainly on agricultural projects that yielded nothing for the coffers of the estate or the fabric of the building. But in his later years he married a rich widow and had money to spend on fixing the Chapel, installing radiators and a telephone system, creating the one bathroom for the Duchess, who paid for it all, and an electricity generator. No more harsh unflattering gaslight!

The First Stateroom was decorated by my great-grandmother, Consuelo Vanderbilt. She sourced and purchased fabrics and furniture in Paris that are still in the rooms today; however, they are gradually being replaced as they have deteriorated with use and sun damage. We are presently recovering sofas and chairs in this room using a similar silk cut-velvet fabric.

We have the 9th Duke and his wealthy American bride to thank for the sudden influx of funds for rescuing Blenheim. Its fabric crumbling, the interior denuded of so many of its treasures and the park looking tired and undisciplined, the Duke set about creating the Italian gardens to the east and the water terraces to west. In the Great Court, the lawns were taken out and terracing and statuary reinstated. Inside, bookcases were removed from Great Library, restoring the architecture. The staterooms were redecorated – perhaps unwisely in a solidly British Baroque building – in the French style, and rooms were once again subject to change of use to suit changing times and family requirements. There were now fewer bedrooms on the principal floor, and the family used the Bow Window Room as their dining room. The Duke was nervous of progress, however, and while he filled the great rooms with art, he did nothing about providing bathrooms.

above The Duchess's Sitting Room is a bit of a hybrid, with much of the decoration from the 9th Duke's era, but the upholstery and the Aubusson rug were recovered and replaced by my father.

opposite The Grand Cabinet is dominated by the rich colours of the magnificent French Savonnerie carpet and fine family portraits. Furniture is from the eighteenth century and covered in fabrics from the 9th Duke's era.

My grandfather, the 10th Duke, conscious of changing expectations, finally bit the bullet with the bathrooms. Not an easy task in a Baroque palace with massively thick walls. Again, rooms changed use. With his large family and often many guests, most of the formal staterooms along the south side were in daily use, as were the rooms beneath the Long Library on the ground floor, which had been interestingly decorated in the era of the 5th Duke. By this time, Blenheim had become a lively family home. The gardens were open to the public for sixpence a head (a little less than fifty cents in US money), and the palace visiting hours were restricted to accommodate family life. Amenities for visitors had also become a consideration.

After my grandfather died in 1972 my father divided his year between Lee Place (my family home as a child) from April to September and Blenheim from October to March. The logic was that he could enjoy privacy during the summer months in a beautiful Georgian house and garden complete with swimming pool, tennis court, croquet lawn, and barbecues, none of which was

possible at Blenheim. During the winter months, when outdoor pursuits such as fox hunting and pheasant shooting were part of the regular calendar of activities, often with a large group of guests staying for two to three days, Blenheim became the ideal base. There were the wonderful original indoor stables close to the house that could accommodate around eight horses and plenty of guest bedrooms – around sixteen – on the second floor.

opposite On the second floor, where all the guest bedrooms are located, the rooms on the east and south side are all interconnected with a generous space in-between to hang clothes and, hopefully, to provide a bit of sound absorption.

above Blenheim was not built with bathrooms in mind so no provision was made for internal drainage, and the solid stone walls make it impossible to retrofit. All the guest bedrooms are interconnected; this bathroom has been created from a dressing room split into two to provide an internal bathroom. Far from glamorous but certainly an upgrade from chamber pots and jugs of hot water.

Always a Problem with Plumbing

The big problem has always been, and still is today, the lack of ensuite bathrooms and plumbing in general. While my grandfather did his best to add a few where possible, the structure and layout of the building made a comprehensive plumbing installation impossible, particularly on the south side of the house where the bedrooms are over the main staterooms. Not only would Historic England not allow it, but there is no way of running pipework under the floors, and so any plumbing and waste pipes had to be snuck into areas often little more than the size of a cupboard.

Since my father passed away in 2014 we have continued to modernise where possible and when funds are available. American guests, in particular, like a good shower, so one new bathroom with a power shower has been installed, and we have plans to create another ensuite, using a room which is currently the housekeeper's storeroom. Covid delayed these plans, and more important restoration projects have jumped the queue.

above left A bathroom cleverly hidden in a cupboard next to the Bachelor three and four bedrooms; fortunately there is a separate loo and wash handbasin in the lobby.

left This suite of two rooms in the mezzanine overlooks the North Courtyard and would have been staff quarters. It now serves as an overflow guest bedroom; it was once used by my brother before the bathroom was installed.

opposite A wash handbasin disguised in an antique cupboard in the Bow Bedroom, which is often used by children. The bathroom is located across the corridor.

Modern Comforts

One of the most frequent complaints from guests was about the uncomfortable old horsehair mattresses. My father's solution was to place boards under the existing mattresses to prevent more sagging and couples colliding into the trough formed in the bed's center. Soon after he died, I arranged to have all the mattresses replaced—and there were a lot of them. This again was not a simple task as none of the ancient four-poster beds were made to modern standard sizes. Thanks to the skills of expert bespoke mattress-makers, however, we now have very happy guests who at breakfast report a blissful night's sleep.

The old, cold stone floors became uneven and unsafe over the centuries. Very threadbare runners were replaced by new carpets on the main staircase in the private East Wing. These were designed incorporating details from the border of one of the tapestries, so they look as if they have been there from the very beginning.

There are also carpets on the piano nobile and in some of the bedrooms. We have updated all the picture lights to LEDs, hopefully saving on electricity bills. Sunlight can cause huge damage to artworks, fabrics and furnishings, so we have installed good quality UV-resistant blinds at all the windows. And there is constant monitoring of the moth population, who love to get their teeth into an old rug or tapestry.

Sharing a home, albeit a palace, with hundreds of thousands of visitors each year does come with its own complications and challenges. To qualify for exemption from certain death duties and because we are open to the public, it means that the private side of the house, notably the East Wing, is required to be on view for a specific number of days of the year. Because my brother does not live there year-round this is not such a problem, but during my father's lifetime it was more complicated, especially during his later years when he had nowhere else to go, and he was forced to entertain only in the evenings and to retreat to areas not on the tour during the day.

At Blenheim, we understand that the visitors' experience needs to be convenient, professional, and memorable so they are happy to return. We are constantly keeping an eye on the complex logistics of moving people around inside the palace, ensuring they get a good view of all our treasures and an understanding of our history. We are aware that this means improving all areas on an annual basis, from adding everyday facilities, updating restaurants and eating places to providing sustainable and disabled access wherever possible in a 300-year-old building so solidly built.

opposite The bedrooms are in much need of an overhaul and the addition of modern facilities, and we are updating them very slowly as funds permit. This one has a lovely view east over the Italian Gardens and so benefits from the morning sun.

left We recently replaced the main stair carpet on the private side from a very threadbare Oriental pattern to this lush red-wool carpet with the border design inspired by the tapestry trim.

This south-facing bedroom had a partial
facelift in 2016 using the existing furniture
but replacing fabrics and some upholstery.

The dressing room attached to the Sunderland Bedroom; the walls and curtains were replaced in the late 1970s by my then stepmother, so they are still in relatively good condition, unlike those in the Tower Bedroom next door.

External paintwork must be kept in good order, metal work needs maintenance, statuary needs cleaning and gates need gilding.

Restoration Challenges

Keeping a 300-year-old building in a state of good repair is a never-ending task. At any one time we have a variety of restoration projects on the go, with a total cost upwards of £40 million, over any ten-year period. Prioritising these works is not easy, and there is always the prospect of unplanned problems needing immediate attention that may force a delay on projects already in the pipeline.

Works are disruptive, too, and it is never palatable to close areas that the public would normally be able to view and enjoy; but thankfully the end results are always well received. Equally frustrating is having to spend huge amounts of money upgrading infra-structure where no visible benefits are seen – rewiring, installing new heating systems, and essential fire-prevention upgrades.

The roof, all three acres of it, is always a priority: gutters, roof lights, and splits in the lead sections are under constant scrutiny. External paintwork must be kept in good order, metalwork maintained, statuary cleaned and gates gilded. My father always claimed that maintenance and repair are the new front line of the battle for Blenheim.

The north facade and portico seen through intricate, partially-gilded metalwork that frames the grand wrought-iron, gilded main entrance gates.

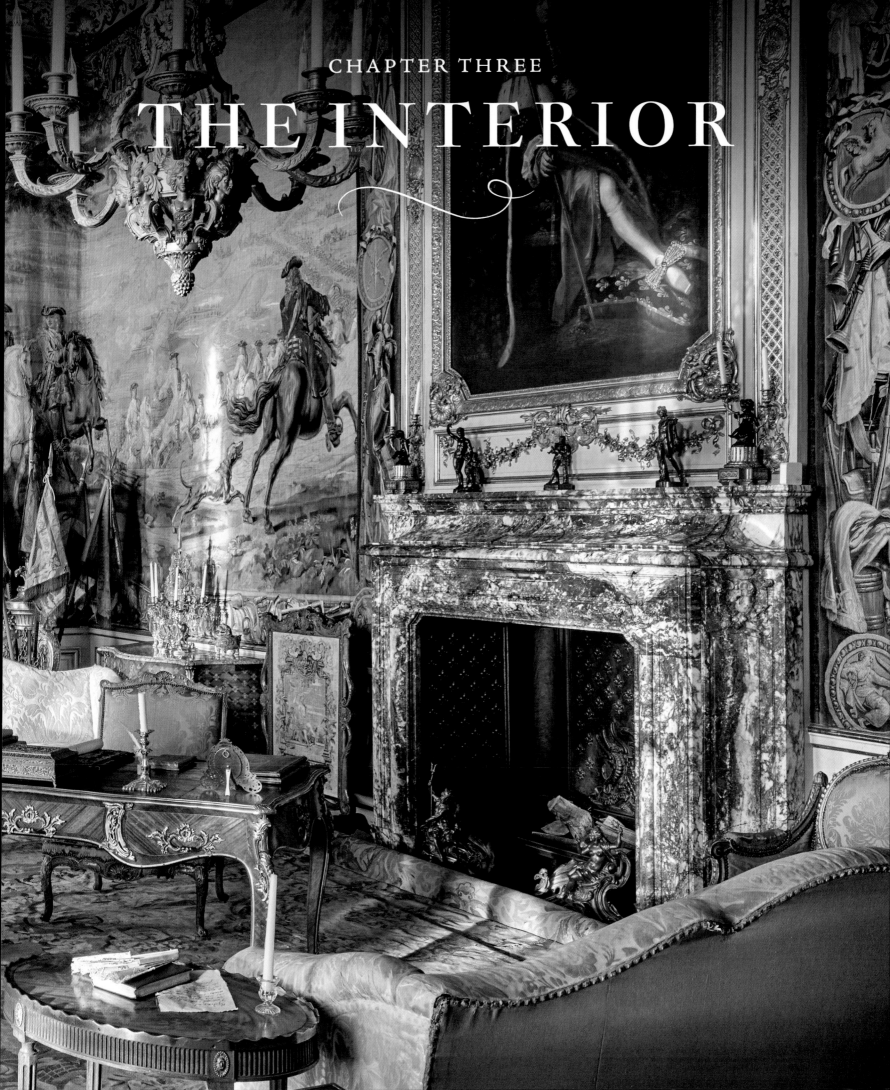

CHAPTER THREE

THE INTERIOR

THE INTERIOR

As well as creating an impressive, monumental palace set in a befitting landscape, there was a massive interior to fit out and decorate, including staterooms, private rooms, colonnades, and corridors. The ornament of the rooms—the plastering, the cornices, the ceilings, murals, fireplaces and doorcases—was always part of Vanbrugh and Hawksmoor's original plan, but, of course, there was a lot of conflicting interference from Sarah, 1st Duchess, who was trying to save money and keep things plain, and from the largely absent Duke, who wanted his monument to be the most magnificent building possible. The stream of priceless art and ornaments, statuary and tapestries sent by the peripatetic Duke to Blenheim from Europe in the course of diplomacy or battle were expected, somehow, to be incorporated into the design. All in all, the pair were an interior designer's nightmare clients.

As the centuries rolled by, fashions changed and new materials and techniques became available. At Blenheim, we have seen all manner of styles—solid Stuart English to gilded French to elegant Georgian to fusty Victorian and, finally, to country house Edwardian—all within the context of a Baroque palace built to stately proportions.

previous pages A portrait of Louis XIV over the fireplace in the Second Stateroom. The tapestry depicts the Siege of Bouchain.

opposite The Great Hall, with its sixty-seven foot (twenty-metre) ceiling. Vanbrugh intended this first impression to be overwhelming.

The inscription below the bust of John Churchill, the 1st Duke, reads in Latin on one side and in English on the other:

Behold the man to distant nations known,
Who shook the Gallick, fix'd the Austrian throne,
New lustre to Britannia's glory gave,
In councils prudent as in action brave.
Not Julius more in arms distinguish'd shin'd,
Nor oud Augustus better calm mankind.

Walls and Ceilings

Sir James Thornhill's original plans for the decoration of the Great Hall envisaged a vast guard room to celebrate Marlborough's military victories. The room is certainly vast at sixty-seven feet high (fifty metres) with elaborate carved-stone cornices, and deep-cut columns with Corinthian capitals supporting the arch and forming a deep ledge from which the windows and ceiling are supported.

The ceiling features an allegorical scene depicting the Duke as Mars in Roman costume sharing the plans of the Battle of Blenheim with Queen Anne as Britannia. The trompe l'oeil and intricate *grisaille* trophy panels flanking the vast windows reprise a heraldic theme, and these did not find favour with Sarah. She felt that Thornhill was taking advantage by charging the same rate for the armorial decoration as he did for the "historical and ornamental" part. There was a dispute about that, as Sarah never let anything slide. Thornhill's bill for the works, dated 1716, amounted to £978, including the *grisaille* (probably carried out by assistants). His itemised bill reads:

for 460 yards 2 foot of Historical and Ornamental Parts of the Ceiling, Mouldings and Coveing at 25 shillings per yard £575.5s – For 321 yards 4 foot more painted with trophy's and Ornaments on the Peers between and under Window there above the Great Cornice at 25 shillings per yard £402 15s Total £987."

That would be about £250,000 in today's money, but I doubt you could get anything like it for that price.

There was much dispute and rethinking of the design for this important area before the Duke, Vanbrugh and Hawksmoor (who generally produced the drawings) settled in 1707 on an agreeable way forward largely fuelled by the Duke's desire to occupy the two main staterooms and the East Wing as soon as feasibly possible. Fearing that the Duke did not have long to enjoy them, Sarah inevitably took control to ensure the two rooms were completed in haste. In the end, as is so often the case, it was the simple expedient of finding the money that got the job done.

Original drawings by Hawksmoor and Vanbrugh depict a much more structurally architectural plan for

left An unexecuted design, dated 1707, for the decoration of the Great Hall, attributed to Hawksmoor and Thornhill.

opposite A view of the Great Hall today, showing that neither the fireplace nor Sir James Thornhill's decorations were ever included.

following pages The painted ceiling in the Saloon by French artist Louis Laguerre. The 1st Duke is depicted in victorious progress but restrained by Peace.

the Saloon, with stone arches and ornamental statues and urns that Thornhill interpreted in some of his original sketches, perhaps a little too similar to the Great Hall.

As it happened, Sarah was displeased with the final cost of Thornhill's work in the Great Hall. As was her nature when she felt she was being exploited, Sarah dismissed his designs and projected costs in favour of the French decorative painter Louis Laguerre, who had trained at Versailles under Charles Le Brun.

Laguerre's execution of the wall paintings is somewhat "bizarre", and to many a critic's eye the random selection of nations from around the world (including a caricature of himself) was perhaps not in keeping with the grandeur of the Grinling Gibbons

marble doorcases. The trompe l'oeil above the marble dado is brilliantly executed and could be taken for any grand, romantic royal palace in Europe. The ceiling, however, looks altogether from a different hand, with a more classical French Baroque style similar to that of Poussin.

above and opposite The trompe l'oeil painting of the ceiling in the Great Hall by Sir James Thornhill that depicts Marlborough presenting the Battle of Blenheim plan to Britannia with *grisaille* wall decorations after a design by Sir James Thornhill.

above Detail from the mural in the Saloon showing the artist Louis Laguerre with Dean Jones, the resident chaplain at the time. It's a signature piece.

opposite The Saloon was frequently used for formal luncheons or dinners. It's an amazing setting, but with stone walls and ceiling, the acoustics are somewhat challenging.

Fireplaces

Many of the fireplaces at Blenheim are relatively simple in terms of style and are designed to be part of the Baroque architecture rather than as a focal point. Certainly, regarding the two in the Saloon, the colour and form of the marble blend in with the walls. Accounts from the contracts for marble works at Blenheim between 1721 and 1723 show charges for both doorcases and raised moulding surrounding the fireplaces.

It is likely that the three fireplaces in the First, Second, and Third Staterooms are the originals as designed by Vanbrugh or Hawskmoor, but those in the Grand Cabinet, Green and Red Drawing Rooms and the Green Writing Room are later additions in a Georgian style that were designed and added in the 1760s by Sir William Chambers at the direction of the 4th Duke.

Bills to the 4th Duke's agent from 1770 for chimney-pieces show:

Thos.Stephens, mason £22 17s 7d
Seffr.Alken, carver £16 3s 2d
Ben. Thacker, joiner £8 0s 0d

In 1772 he provides a drawing for the Duchess's Dressing Room chimneypiece stating "the frieze and panels of the Pilasters may be of any other colour, as green or red." In the East Wing there are some important early fire surrounds designed by Vanbrugh or Hawksmoor and carved by Grinling Gibbons, notably in the East Wing Bow Window Room (now the family Dining Room) and the Duchess's Bedchamber next door. Ironically, there is also one in the undercroft, now staff quarters, incorporating a two-foot coronet carved in stone.

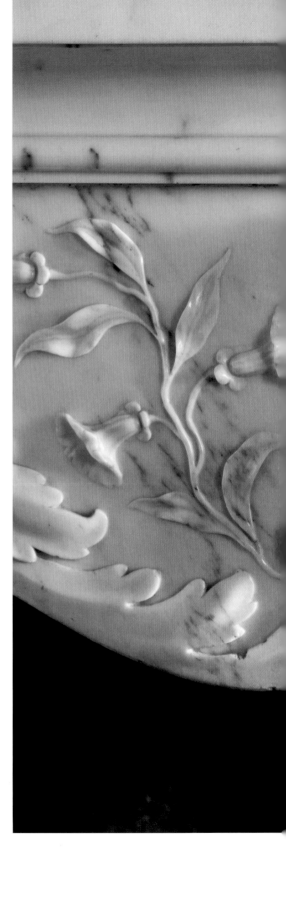

previous pages, left One of a pair of matching marble fireplaces, designed to be simple and architectural to blend in with the rest of the room.

previous pages, right Fire surround in the Red Drawing Room designed by William Chambers, c. 1775, and executed by Joseph Wilton.

opposite and above The c. 1750 fire surround in the Green Drawing Room, in Carrara marble. The tapered jambs are carved with scallop shells and the centre carving depicting a mask of Flora, goddess of flowers and springtime.

opposite An early eighteenth-century white marble fire surround in the Bow Window Room (now the family's private dining room).

right An early eighteenth-century white marble fire surround in the Duchess's bedroom, designed by Sir John Vanbrugh and carved by Grinling Gibbons.

One of a pair of early-Georgian Palladian-style fire surrounds in the Long Library, dated around 1733, and possibly designed by Sir William Kent. The elaborate carved overmantels are part of the plasterwork designed by Hawksmoor.

In the Green Writing Room, a George
III Carrara-and-black-marble fire
surround with a central tablet carved
with a Bacchic mask. This would have
been added by the 4th Duke.

left Four identical massive marble doorcases that were originally commissioned to be carved by Grinling Gibbons; however, only one was completed before works stopped in 1712, and the remaining three were completed by others. The crest is the 1st Duke's armorial, and it shows the double-headed eagle of the Holy Roman Empire.

opposite One of many pairs of double mahogany doors with raised and fielded panels showing a fluted detail repeated in the architraves. Very elegant.

Doorcases

The most imposing doorcases are the four marble ones in the Saloon designed by Vanbrugh. The original one was carved by Grinling Gibbons in 1712 before work stopped for four years. Sadly, Gibbons never returned to complete the other three, which were then carved by another hand. The deep reveals are flanked by square columns that act as the architraves, and the arched head is surmounted by a huge shell scroll. Within the arch is the armorial of the 1st Duke with the double-headed eagle, the crest of the Holy Roman Empire. The Duke was created Prince of the Holy Roman empire in 1704.

The Long Library was the last room to be completed (as Vanbrugh worked from east to west, acknowledging the Duke's wishes to be able to live in the house sooner rather than later). Originally planned to be a picture gallery, the interior ended up being designed by Hawksmoor (although he never saw it to fruition) as Vanbrugh had been dismissed by this stage by the volatile Duchess. Hawksmoor's design, executed between 1723 and 1725, sensibly divided the long room of 180 feet (fifty-five metres) into a sequence of spaces with intricate architectural details in the arches, pilasters and plaster mouldings that resulted in an extremely elegantly proportioned room that could serve many functions. The marble doorcase opposite the bow window is a triumphant focal point, creating a view right through colonnades and the Great Hall to the Bow Window Room on the east side (the view is now boarded up, so it is not possible to appreciate the original perspective). The double mahogany doors would have been added during the 4th Duke's time. As in most other examples in the house, the doorcase forms an integral part of the internal architecture of the room, with gilded carved-wood details for added flourish.

left An impressive enfilade through three sets of mahogany double doors from the Third Stateroom to the First. It is said that the doors are so perfectly aligned that you could see from east to west through the keyholes.

right The imposing marble doorcase was designed by Hawksmoor and carved by William Townsend and Bartholomew Peisley, a local master stonemason.

Awe-inspiring entrance

The massive front door, carved from solid oak, is set into a portico designed by Vanbrugh specifically to overwhelm and intimidate the visitor with its "castle-like" air. The elaborate lock is a copy of the lock on the gates to Warsaw and bears the motto *Dieu Defend Le Droit*. The door opens only from the inside, so it is not very practical; however, there is a smaller inset door that cleverly encompasses the two lower panels to disguise it for daily use (although not ideally as it requires stepping over the base stile). The family entrance to the private side is on the left, or east, side.

Plasterwork

opposite and above The magnificent Long Library, originally planned to be a picture gallery, has intricate plasterwork designed by Hawksmoor and executed by Isaac Mansfield. The room was converted into a library by the 3rd Duke to house his father's extensive collection of books and manuscripts. The room is split into sections to create individual usable areas. The ceiling panels were originally designed to have murals by Thornhill, but sadly they were never executed.

following pages Intricate plasterwork detail in an oval shape that radiates out from a central scrollwork and sunburst medallion.

Much of the elaborate plasterwork as seen today was designed by Sir Nicholas Hawksmoor and stayed intact even after Sir William Chambers had been commissioned by the 4th Duke to bring the house in line with the fashions of the day. Chambers sensibly decided to leave much of the original interior architecture intact.

Some of the most intricate work is in the Long Library, where stucco work was carried out in the two false domes on the south and north ends by Isaac Mansfield (a well-known master plasterer who worked on churches with Hawksmoor). Once the Willis organ was moved from its central bay-window position in 1902 to the North Bay, the room lost its symmetry; however, the magnificent organ now creates an impressive focal point at the end of this very long room.

above The Upper Gallery is at the south
end of the room behind the bust of Queen
Anne and accessed through a small hidden
staircase. Today, it houses less exclusive but
nonetheless relevant volumes.

above right The organ by Henry Willis was commissioned by the 8th Duke in 1891. It was originally placed in the central bow window, but was moved eleven years later to the north end.

following pages The elaborate plasterwork in this First Stateroom is not the original by Hawksmoor but altered to be more French in the Victorian Rococo style and more in keeping with the grandness of Versailles, with the fleur-de-lys in the corner decoration.

left The main bedroom in the private apartments of the East Wing. The original plasterwork was by Hawksmoor but embellished by Sir William Chambers in the 1760s. In the centre of the corner decoration is the Ducal Crown, with a double M for Marlborough.

opposite The Green Writing Room has an original Hawksmoor ceiling. The corner crests were added around 1890 with the Churchill crest and the Garter crests, which read *"Honi Soit Qui Mal Y Pense"* or "Shame on he who thinks ill of it."

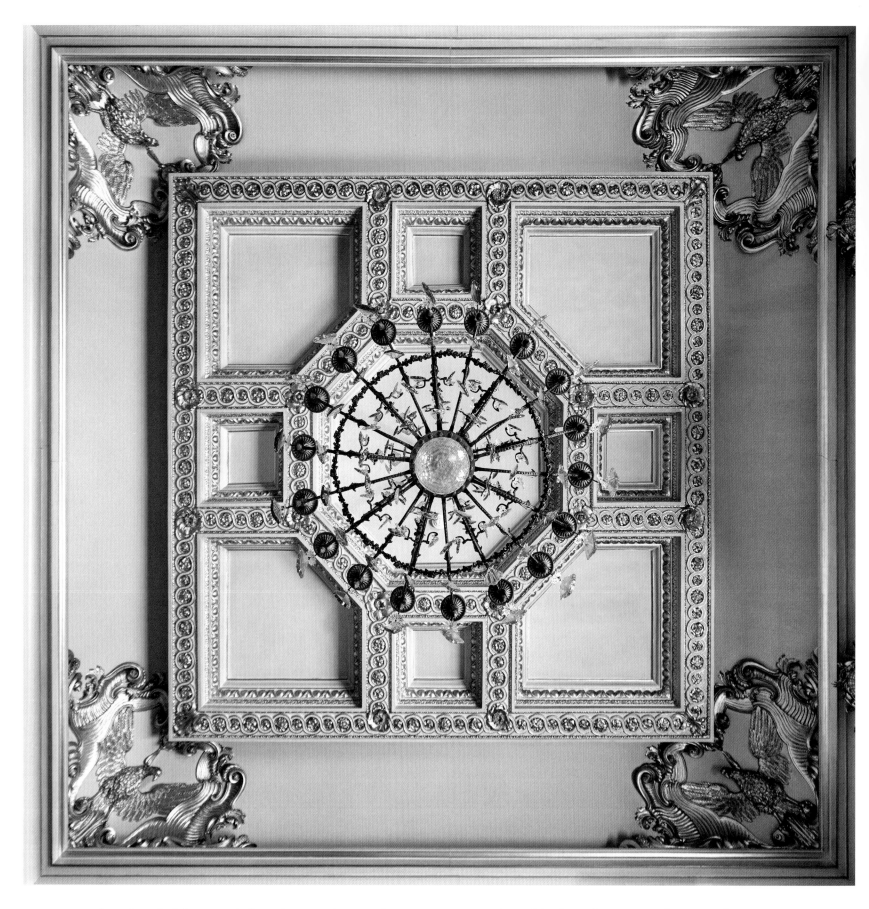

above Detail of the original Green Drawing Room ceiling designed by Nicholas Hawksmoor. The deep coving allows for a deep central block of detailed symmetrical gilded plasterwork, giving an impression of height.

opposite One of the five ceiling areas in the Long Library designed by Hawksmoor but executed by Isaac Mansfield. The two at each end have a coffered dome with an octagonal shape surrounded by clerestory windows.

Paintings and Artwork

Sadly, important artworks have inevitably come and gone from Blenheim over the past 300 years – some intentionally, some through forced sales and some by pure misfortune.

John Churchill, the 1st Duke, had commissioned Flemish tapestries to depict his numerous victories over the French, but he soon realised from his visits to many other royal residences in England, Paris, Vienna and beyond that Blenheim required art suitable in quality and recognition to adorn the walls of a palace. What is more, his son-in-law, now the 3rd Earl of Sunderland, who had married his second daughter, Anne, had a far superior art collection. John was a lover of the arts and between his various battles he found time to purchase some fine paintings by Rubens and Van Dyke, while paintings by other illustrious artists were gifted by the Emperor of Germany and the Cities of Antwerp and Brussels.

PAINTINGS

The 1st Duke commissioned family portraits by Closterman, Charles Jervas, and Godfrey Kneller. The most historical and important of the Closterman paintings is the family group painted in 1693. The

setting is suitably grand, with architectural detail and a landscape in the distance, yet the whole composition is softened by lush, draped curtains and lavish gowns for the Duchess and her four daughters. Ironically, it is Anne, the second daughter, who stands out from the crowd in her red dress, and it is she from whom we are all descended, as it was her son, Charles, who became the 3rd Duke.

In the Green Writing Room (originally the Dining Room in the early eighteenth century) hangs Godfrey Kneller's fine portrait of John Churchill in his suit of armour. By the time John moved into Blenheim, it served as a poignant reminder to the ailing Duke of his vigorous past. Having suffered a stroke, John stood in front of the painting just before he died and commented "that was once a man."

According to records, John wrote to Sarah in November 1706 setting out his intention to bring back works of art to furnish the Gallery at Blenheim. These included Van Dyke's equestrian portrait of King Charles, possibly *Lot and his Daughter* by Rubens, as well as other Rubens and Titians for which the Duke had a particular penchant. One gift from the Duke of Savoy was a group of nine oils on leather by Titian, known as *The Loves of the Gods*. These originally hung in the Great Hall and eventually moved to a room next to the theatre (now the Orangery), firstly so they could be viewed by paying visitors, secondly because the 7th Duke, being deeply religious and a bit of a prude, considered them too raunchy to be on display to family and friends. Unfortunately, in 1861 a fire broke out in the adjacent kitchens and the Titians, along with other artworks, were destroyed.

opposite The majority of the walls in the palace are either hung with tapestries or family portraits from the early eighteenth century to today, although, sadly, photography has rather taken over from traditional portraits.

left Caroline, the 4th Duchess of Marlborough, and her daughter by Sir Joshua Reynolds.

following pages The Grand Cabinet on the south-east corner displays many beautiful family portraits and miniatures. Over the fireplace is Caroline, 4th Duchess, by George Romney. To the left is a paintng of the Spencer children – Charles, Robert, Anne, and John – by Godfrey Kneller.

The 7th Duke, being deeply religious and a bit of a prude, considered the Titians too raunchy to be on display to family and friends.

BACCHUS & ARIADNE.

Inventories from the Duchess dated 1740 list paintings acquired for both Marlborough House in London and for Blenheim, possibly many of them stored at Marlborough House temporarily while Blenheim was being completed. Following the Duchess's death, most of the artworks passed to John Spencer, her favourite grandson, and so ended up at the Spencer seat at Althorp. When Charles Spencer, John's older brother, succeeded as 3rd Duke of Marlborough, he added bookcases to house his father's great library, so the gallery no longer had the wall space to accommodate so many works of art.

Subsequent dukes commissioned the obligatory family portraits from the fashionable artists of the

time, as well as others relevant to their specific interests or travels. The 3rd Duke, Charles Spencer, whose home before becoming duke was Langley Park in Buckinghamshire, had already commissioned Venetian views by Canaletto. He also had a love of horses, and John Wootton, the English hunting and landscape painter, supplied many horse portraits as well as a series of canvases for the hall at Althorp. While Charles spent little time at Blenheim, he appreciated and respected his grandmother's arrangements and so made few changes.

The 4th Duke had money to spend, and his plans to entertain on a grand scale required the rooms to be furnished accordingly. He had inherited some superb works of art, and he commissioned family portraits by

Sir Joshua Reynolds; the main one, dated 1778, now hangs in the Red Drawing Room. Reynold's painting depicts the Duke's family with the Duke in his Garter robes, his wife and her towering hairdo at the centre, and an artful grouping of his six children. The scene is not dissimilar to that of the 1st Duke's family portrait by Closterman, with its grand architectural backdrop and view beyond, softened with drapery and the lavish costumes of the day. The Duke is holding one of the sardonyx gems from the cameo collection and his son and heir holds a crimson case containing more gems. The delightful scene also hints at the family's love of amateur dramatics.

Over the fireplace in the Green Drawing Room hangs a fine painting of the 4h Duke by George Romney, dated 1779, and another by Joshua Reynolds of his young wife, Caroline, and one of their young children.

George Scharf's comprehensive catalogue raisonné from 1862 shows which paintings were hanging in which rooms from that time, and while most of the rooms have been renamed and are largely open to the public,

it makes for depressing reading to see how few great paintings other than family portraits remain today.

Much to his brother Lord Randolph's horror and protestations, the 8th Duke was responsible for selling off many of Blenheim's most important works, some of which had survived until his time. Van Dyke's *Charles 1* went to the National Gallery for £17,500, Raphael's *Ansidei Madonna* for £70,000, and an auction at Christie's over five days amassed £400,000. That's over £60 million in today's money.

opposite Pages from the portfolio of engravings featuring the erotic Titian leather wall hangings *Loves of the Gods* that were destroyed by fire.

below The plan of the Piano Nobile, which relates to George Scharf's *Catalogue Raisonné* of 1862, in which each painting of merit was listed room by room.

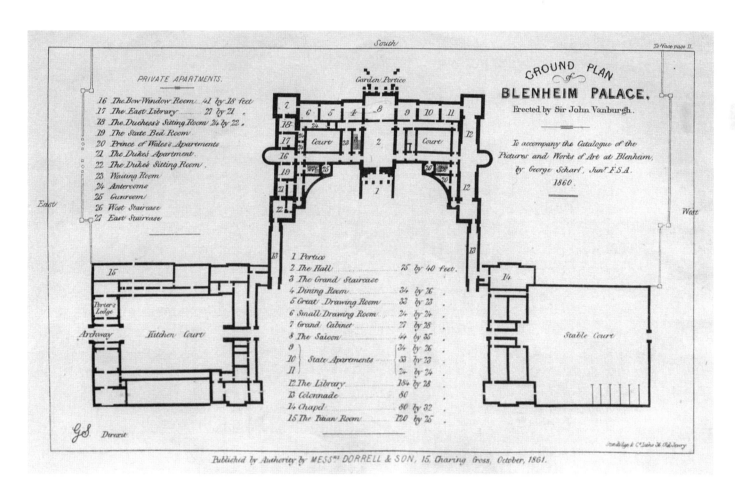

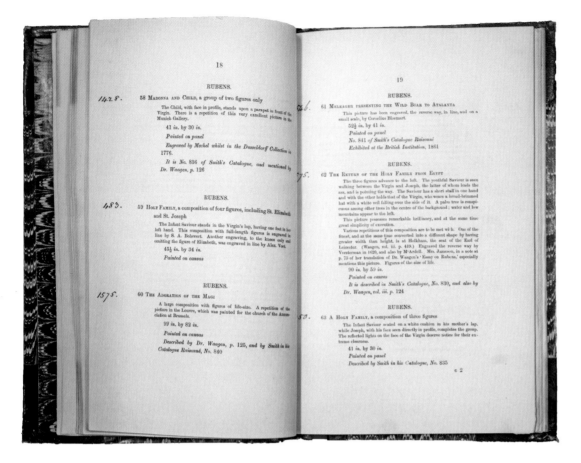

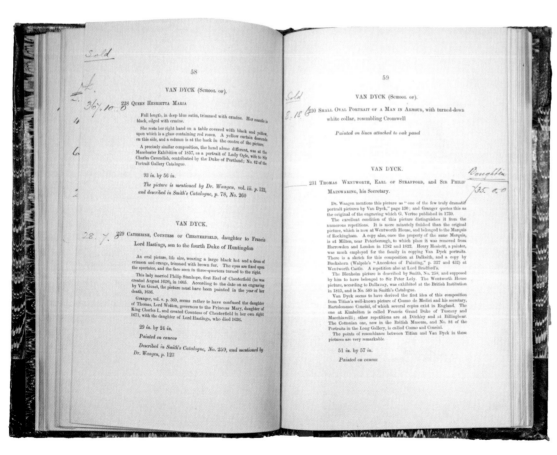

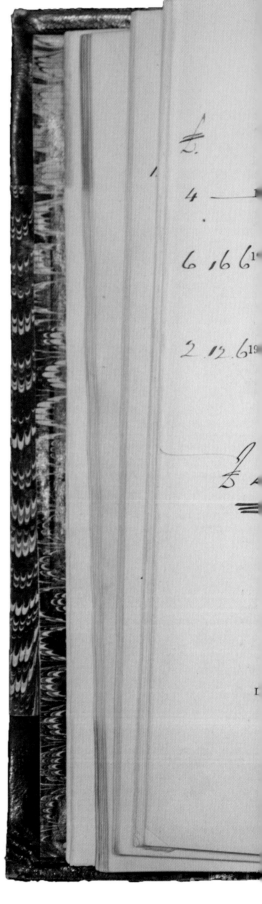

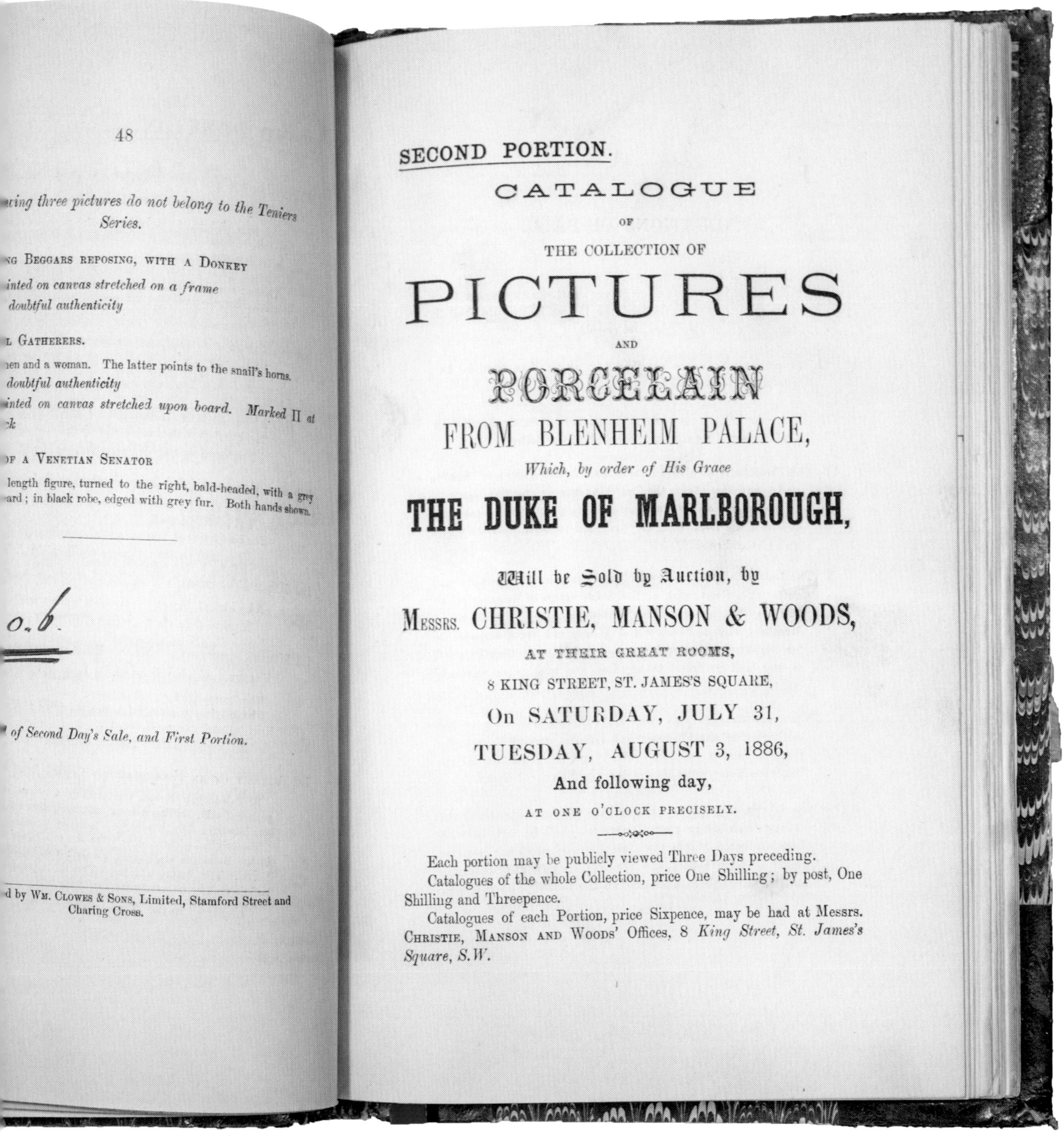

...wing three pictures do not belong to the Teniers
Series.

...NG BEGGARS REPOSING, WITH A DONKEY
...inted on canvas stretched on a frame
...doubtful authenticity

...L GATHERERS.
...en and a woman.   The latter points to the snail's horns.
...doubtful authenticity
...inted on canvas stretched upon board.   Marked II at
...k

...OF A VENETIAN SENATOR
...length figure, turned to the right, bald-headed, with a grey
...ard ; in black robe, edged with grey fur.   Both hands shown.

o.b.

...of Second Day's Sale, and First Portion.

...d by WM. CLOWES & SONS, Limited, Stamford Street and
Charing Cross.

SECOND PORTION.

CATALOGUE

OF

THE COLLECTION OF

PICTURES

AND

PORCELAIN

FROM BLENHEIM PALACE,

Which, by order of His Grace

THE DUKE OF MARLBOROUGH,

Will be Sold by Auction, by

MESSRS. CHRISTIE, MANSON & WOODS,

AT THEIR GREAT ROOMS,

8 KING STREET, ST. JAMES'S SQUARE,

On SATURDAY, JULY 31,

TUESDAY, AUGUST 3, 1886,

And following day,

AT ONE O'CLOCK PRECISELY.

Each portion may be publicly viewed Three Days preceding.
Catalogues of the whole Collection, price One Shilling ; by post, One
Shilling and Threepence.
Catalogues of each Portion, price Sixpence, may be had at Messrs.
CHRISTIE, MANSON AND WOODS' Offices, 8 *King Street, St. James's
Square, S.W.*

Pages from the sale catalogue listing the numerous valuable
works of art and some of the prices raised for them. These
treasures were sold by the 8th Duke in 1896 at the auction
house Christie, Manson and Woods.

Miniatures

Early miniature portraits date from the sixteenth century. Previously etched in books or documents, these small treasures became prized as keepsakes and generous gifts set into lockets, boxes or elaborate frames. The trend in England evolved from France, and many artists took inspiration from large portraiture, painting miniatures in watercolour on vellum. As the technique developed, artists progressed to painting on enamel and ivory, which was more complex because the nonabsorbent surface was harder to control. In the Blenheim collection many are framed in oval or round frames as a group. During the nineteenth century, artists began to paint larger individual portraits, which allowed them to be hung directly onto the wall. We were lucky to be able to acquire many of those seen here from the estate of Victor Churchill, a descendant of the 4th Duke.

The 9th Duke was nervous of progress ... and while he filled the great rooms with art, he did nothing about providing bathrooms.

Capturing a way of life

Rather sadly, in my view, fewer portraits are painted since the advent of photography, and since the explosion of digital photography so many images are destined to sit forever on a phone or in a computer and will never make their way into curated and annotated albums.

I am very fond of portraits and paintings that depict a way of life, whether sporting or entertaining, and many wonderful artists from the eighteenth, nineteenth and twentieth centuries were commissioned by the aristocracy to do just that. The 1st Duke bought horse paintings by the fashionable sporting artist John Wootton and series of them hang in the Smoking Room. Wootton was replaced by the more fashionable George Stubbs and in the same room we are lucky to have one of his more exotic paintings of a tiger.

The 9th Duke was an accomplished horseman, as was Consuelo, and part of their time was spent in

Leicestershire, renowned for its great hunting grounds. He commissioned Sir Alfred James Munnings to paint him and his second son, Lord Ivor, out in the field as they changed over to their second horses. My father, too, loved to foxhunt and hanging over the entrance to the bar area on the private side is a delightful portrait of him and my stepmother, Rosita, very much in the Munnings style, but by La Fontaine.

above Hunting with the hounds and riding has always been a way of life in English country houses and, as depicted in these two paintings, our family is no exception.

opposite This wonderful painting of a tiger by George Stubbs was commissioned by the 4th Duke. It is said to be the tigress gifted to the Duke by Lord Clive, Governor of Bengal. Above it is the 3rd Duke and Charles Vane by John Wootton.

Painting the Belle Epoque

During the late nineteenth and early twentieth centuries, society was spoilt for choice, with fashionable and talented artists eager to paint the beautiful society ladies of the Belle Epoque and the European elite. Many of them studied and worked in France but travelled extensively to fulfil commissions. Undoubtably, John Singer Sargent was the king of this genre, and although his parents were American, he was born in Florence and spent most of his life in Paris and London.

My great-grandmother was American and she and her mother, Alva, visited Paris often, and I am sure that influenced the many beautiful portraits by the artists who painted her. Her engagement portrait by Emile Auguste Carolus-Duran, commissioned by her mother when she was just seventeen, hangs over the fireplace in the First Stateroom; I have to admit she looks pretty forlorn as the setting depicts her future life as a duchess. A more favourable portrait is that by Ambrose McEvoy, which hangs in a corridor off the Great Hall. But my two favourites are the Umberto Veruda that hangs outside the pantry on the private side and makes a wonderful focal point as it draws your eye down the corridor, and the recently acquired pastel by Paul César Helleu, painted when he stayed in 1900, showing off her fine features and long neck.

Veruda also painted my great-grandfather in his red hunting coat and had they remained married to one another, I suspect the two portraits would have been displayed together. When he finally got divorced, having been separated for many years, Sunny married his longtime friend Gladys Deacon, who was considered one of the most beautiful and charming of society ladies and who was friendly with the likes of Manet and Proust. The stunning Boldini portrait of her was painted five years before she and Sunny married, and we are fortunate to have reacquired it, completing a wonderful set of Belle Epoque artists.

above My beautiful great-grandmother Consuelo Vanderbilt, by Paul César Helleu in pastel. The elegant translucent outfit shows off her slim physique and the choker emphasises her long neck.

opposite On the easel is the 9th Duke's second wife, Gladys Deacon, by Giovanni Boldini. Painted in 1901, Gladys was another French American society lady and a friend of Consuelo's before becoming his second wife. On the wall behind the easel is Consuelo again, this time painted by Ambrose McEvoy.

VERUDA

Charles Spencer-Churchill
Duke of Marlborough - 1903

Sketches and drawings

When my brother and I were young, my mother had us sketched by various talented local artists. I have copies of these, but neither James and his family nor myself have to date had serious portraits painted, which is a shame as they really are such a lasting and romantic way of telling family history and certainly enhance any room setting.

When my father was married to Tina (née Livanos), she introduced the family to the Spanish artist Alejo Vidal-Quadras, who had a prolific career in Europe and South America producing works from still-life oils to pastel landscapes and portraits in oil, pastel, and charcoal. Our family ones are all charcoal. I have always loved the picture of me and James painted in 1962 when I was five and he eight. We have several of the three generations, which now hang at Blenheim.

opposite Three personal family portraits of my great-grandfather, the 9th Duke, and his two sons Bert and Ivor, painted by Umberto Veruda, an Austrian-Hungarian who was born in Trieste and studied in Munich and Paris. These date from 1903.

right and below Family sketches by Alejo Vidal-Quadras.

John Piper at Blenheim

As far as contemporary art is concerned, we have never invested in such works, mainly because we prefer to concentrate our resources on reacquiring lost works. Also, the prices are just too high, and we don't have the wall space to do them justice. I guess the most recent acquisitions were a set of John Piper landscapes depicting various scenes of the palace and gardens in his distinct naturalistic pen-and-ink style. They sit very comfortably in the main corridor on the Piano Nobile on the East Wing.

left The Lower Water Terrace created by the 9th Duke between 1925 and 1931.

above A 1970s triptych of the Grand Bridge from various angles in pen and coloured ink.

What is most remarkable about the tapestries at Blenheim is that they have remained on permanent display for the past 300 years undisturbed.

Tapestries

So many historic tapestries were treated with carelessness, ending up threadbare, faded and damaged with nails as they were carted from draughty, damp residence to draughty, damp residence as a reminder to all and sundry of the rank and wealth of the noble owner. What is most remarkable about the tapestries at Blenheim is that they have remained on permanent display for the past 300 years undisturbed, apart from necessary cleaning and restoration work. For all his tapestry commissions, the 1st Duke was insistent that the weaving and materials were of the highest quality available, and that is why today the scenes are so fresh and the colours still so vibrant.

The first tapestries destined for Blenheim were the *Art of War* series, a set of nine. These tapestries were, in a way, off-the-peg. This beautifully designed series, glorifying military might, textbook tactics, and the splendour of battle was created in 1696 for the Elector of Bavaria. The Flemish tapestry dealer Nicolaas Naulaerts saw the potential of these popular themes, and he oversaw commissions for seven sets to adorn various castles and palaces in Europe – and one of the seven was destined for Blenheim. The 1st Duke ordered his set in 1706 when Blenheim Palace was still a building site and a set of plans, so he was not able to get exact measurements for the hanging spaces in the East Wing (which was fast-tracked to be habitable). He went ahead despite this, and the workshops set about adapting the design and weaving the panels, charging extra for adding a portrait of the Duke and specially designed borders featuring the Duke's coat of arms. Some of the panels did not fit and had to be folded over at the bottom (a tapestry will unravel if it's cut), and the border was used to cover up the miscalculation.

The Duke also acquired a set of *Alexander Tapestries* woven by the Flemish master weaver Josse de Vos from original works by Charles Le Brun. These depicted triumphant scenes from the legendary life of Alexander the Great. Several sets of these seven panels were made. One is at Blenheim, and there is also a set in the Queen's Gallery at Hampton Court.

The *Victories* set of tapestries for the staterooms at Blenheim was the 1st Duke's most ambitious and expensive commission. There were to be eleven panels depicting his victories over the armies of Louis XIV, and a twelfth panel depicting peace. All the designs were impressively correct in their depictions of terrain and battle formations and portraits of the people involved – a huge, costly but splendid undertaking. At the same time, weavers were working on another set of four *Virtues* to celebrate John Churchill's appointment as Prince of the Holy Roman Empire. All this stunning imagery was commissioned once the palace walls could be correctly measured and prepared with plain panelled areas to exactly accept each panel. The Flemish weavers were kept very busy for many years.

Tapestry mania could only go so far. Vanbrugh was preparing wainscoted panels for the Grand Cabinet, the Great Hall and the Long Gallery, but the Duke intervened. These rooms were to be for displaying "the finest pictures he could obtain," along with mirrors and statuary.

left A tapestry from the Alexander series dating from the early eighteenth century. Alexander the Great is depicted in a chariot as he makes his triumphal entry into Babylon. Since Blenheim has been open to the public, the rooms are subject to extra traffic and dust, so conservators have ensured the light levels are kept down to keep the environment as stable as possible.

following pages Setting the scene for the family dining room are tapestries from the *Art of War* series woven in Brussels by Jerome Le Clerc and Jacques van der Borght. In the beginning, tapestries were attached to the walls of the palace with hooks and rings. In the 1930s the hooks and rings were gradually replaced by press studs. Today, the press studs are being replaced with Velcro strips.

left Two more tapestries from the Alexander series, on the left: Alexander meeting Chaldean prophets on his way to Babylon and, on the right, Alexander and Diogenes.

following pages One of the tapestries from the *Victories* series commissioned by John Churchill to illustrate his famous victories during the War of Spanish Succession (1701–1714). This one tells of the Battle of Malplaquet in 1709.

above and opposite Details from tapestries that hang in the Sunderland Bedroom, which are part of the four *Virtues* set depicting Temperance (*left*), Fortitude (*right*), Justice and Prudence. Each shows the duke's coat of arms as a prince of the Holy Roman Empire.

To
The Memory
of
QUEEN ANN
Under Whose Auspices
JOHN DUKE of MARLBOROUGH
Conquered
And to Whose Munificence
He And His Posterity
with Gratitude
Owe the Posfefsion
of
BLENHEIM
A: D: MDCCXXXX VI

Sculpture

From the 1st Duke and Duchess's era, the works of John Michael Rysbrack are significant pieces. The somewhat flattering sculpture of Queen Anne in the southern end of the Long Library (originally planned to be in the Bow Window Room in the private East Wing) was something of an afterthought and a benevolent gesture from Sarah to honour the Queen to whom she owed much of her wealth and success. In pure white marble, the sculpture is a delicate and dignified work, showing a slimmed-down Anne in regal robes.

Sarah stated that the statue should cost no more than £300, commenting to her favourite granddaughter, Diana, "that she would have satisfaction in showing this respect to her, because her kindness to me was real. And what happened afterwards was compassed by the contrivance of such as are in power now."

The inscription reads:

To The Memory of Queen Anne under whose auspices John Duke of Marlborough conquered and to whose munificence He and His Posterity With Gratitude Owe the Possession of Blenheim
A:D:MDCCXXXX:VI

The base was designed by Sir William Chambers and it rightly elevates the statue to work with the height of the Long Library, with the Queen looking down on her subjects. Also in the Long Library is a Rysbrack bust of the 1st Duke, again on a Chambers pedestal, now in the bow window; and another of Charles Spencer, Earl of Sunderland, which is placed over one of the fireplaces. A further bust of Marlborough sits above the marble doorcase from the Great Hall to the Saloon and is reputed to be by Rysbrack or most probably by one of his masters, such as Ven der Voort (described in Sarah's inventory as "done by a famous man from Antwerp.")

Of course, the most significant sculpture by Rysbrack is the Marlborough tomb in the Chapel. Hawksmoor produced a proposal, but it was William Kent, the up-and-coming architect at the time, who won the contract. The Duke died in 1722, and although it was his wish to be buried in the Chapel at Blenheim, neither the Chapel nor tomb were completed until 1733, so his body was laid in Westminster Abbey until such time it could be moved. The end result, which came in on budget at £2,200, was as Sarah wished, depicting her beloved husband as a victorious hero along with herself and their two sons, both of whom had died in infancy. Either side of the sarcophagus are two large statues representing History with her quill and Fame with her trumpet.

opposite Displayed at the south end of the Long Library this is very much a tribute statue of Queen Anne, commissioned from Michael Rysbrack as a gesture of goodwill and gratitude from Sarah, the 1st Duchess, following her husband's death.

left Charles Spencer, who became the 3rd Duke in 1733, by Michael Rysbrack.

TO THE MEMORY
OF
IOHN
DVKE OF
MARLBOROVGH
AND HIS TWO SONS.
SARAH
HIS DVCHESS
HAS ERECTED THIS
MONVMENT
IN THE YEAR OF CHRIST
MDCCXXXIII.

TO THE MEMORY
OF
IOHN
DVKE OF
MARLBOROVGH
AND HIS TWO SONS.
SARAH
HIS DVCHESS
HAS ERECTED THIS
MONVMENT
IN THE YEAR OF CHRIST
MDCCXXXIII.

opposite and above In the Chapel, a fitting memorial to John
Churchill commissioned by Sarah after his death, designed by
William Kent and sculpted by Michael Rysbrack. It depicts
John as a victorious hero in a Roman general's costume and is
also a tribute to their two sons who died at a young age. A detail
(*above*) shows History with her quill.

above A pair of busts of John and Frances,
the 7th Duke and Duchess of Marlborough by
Lawrence Macdonald.

opposite A portrait bust of Consuelo,
9th Duchess of Marlborough.

TWENTIETH-CENTURY SCULPTURE

Winston Churchill's international fame attracted
attention and consequently many sculpture commissions. We have an example at Blenheim of Jacob
Epstein's magnificent bronze and also the Epstein busts
of Winston's cousin, the 9th Duke, and his son, my
great-uncle Ivor. Oscar Nemon, who created the bronze
now in the Churchill Garden, also crafted Clementine
and Winston together in their old age in a sculpture he
titled *Married Love*.

above Winston and Clementine.

opposite Charles, the 9th Duke, and his son, Ivor (*right*),
by Epstein in 1925 and 1931.

CAROLVS · MM · DVX · MCMXXV

Silver

There is spectacular silver at Blenheim, some on display in staterooms and some used on a semi-regular basis; the rest is stored in our vaults but rotated on display for people to admire.

One of my all-time favourite pieces is the Garrard Centrepiece of the 1st Duke. Commissioned during the Victorian period, the 7th Duke's tenure, the piece is normally displayed in the Saloon. It depicts Marlborough on horseback writing battle plans, or his famous dispatch to his Duchess, on a kettle drum surrounded by attendants. The theme seems to have been taken from one of the tapestries, and it is certainly a talking point.

Much of the silver is shared between the private and public areas of the house, and depending on the occasion, a formal black-tie dinner or less formal lunch, there are items to suit. On evening formal occasions, the table is set using the same fiddle thread and shell cutlery set. These are typical of the Georgian era, so it is assumed that they were largely purchased by the 4th Duke but no doubt added to subsequently, as different maker's marks exist. This supports the Churchill Crest (a lion) and the Ducal Coronet.

In the Saloon, the pair of seven-light candelabra by Edward Barnard are silver gilt and dated 1855 (the company dates from 1680). They would have been commissioned by the 7th Duke and engraved with Spencer-Churchill armorials in the flamboyant scrolling style of the Victorian period.

Other silver-gilt pieces consist of a suite of six Victorian comports – two double-tiered on scrolling circular bases decorated with foliage and Gothic strapwork details and four single-tiered to match. Depending on the length of the table, two to six will be used to display fresh fruit, dried fruit, and chocolate.

For flower displays, there are silver-gilt verrières, a pair of George III bowls by Magdalen Feline are dated 1763, so these would have been commissioned by the 4th Duke. A later set of four Victorian monteith bowls on stands showing both Spencer-Churchill and Galloway crests tell us that they would have been commissioned by the 5th Duke when he was married to Susan, the daughter of the Earl of Galloway.

Monteith bowls (or verrières, the later versions) were originally intended to cool wineglasses in iced water, and the notches around the edges held the stems. Today they are more commonly used as a type of low flower container and perfect for a table setting. They are especially useful if lined with glass and filled with oasis.

It was typical to decant fine wine, and the tradition dates backs to the late seventeenth century, when wine would have been decanted from a larger amphora to be more easily handled. The tradition continues as a practical way to separate the liquid from the sediment, and decanting allows old wine to breathe before being served. Most of the decanters at Blenheim date from the Victorian era and have elaborate scrollwork with trailing vines.

Other more decorative pieces include chargers and alms dishes dating from the 1st and 4th Duke's tenures.

above A nineteenth-century electroplated equestrian model of the 1st Duke.

opposite A magnificent centrepiece of the 1st Duke by British heritage jeweller Garrard.

opposite One of a set of four Victorian monteiths on stands by Charles Stuart Harris, c. 1896.

above Detail showing the family crest on one of many silver chargers that are used on a regular basis.

Porcelain

The bulk of the fine porcelain at Blenheim was gifted and how fortunate we were to be recipients of such fine collections. While the 3rd Duke spent a limited time living at Blenheim, preferring Langley Park, he was no doubt well-known among the royal circles of Europe, having spent time in the army. Somewhere during these trips, perhaps while hunting, he must have encountered the king of Poland, who had a passion for hunting and was keen to have a pack of English staghounds. The British envoy at the time, Sir Charles Hanbury Williams, brokered a deal and in return for a pack of hounds the Duke was gifted a fine Meissen dinner service. Another fine set of Sèvres porcelain, presumably another gift or purchase from travels in Europe by the 3rd or 4th Dukes, is also housed in the China Ante Room outside the Green Drawing Room.

During the 4th Duke's period, his wife, Caroline, received a letter from an anonymous owner of a very substantial collection of Chinese and Japanese porcelain acquired over his lifetime, suggesting that if the circumstances were appropriate, he would consider gifting the collection to Blenheim. His reason for the gift was that he wanted the set to be kept together and available for others to enjoy in suitable surroundings.

His original suggestion was that the Duke and Duchess should build a pagoda-style building on the grounds to house the collection on one floor so it could be displayed harmoniously and themed. He also implied that perhaps he might be employed to look after the collection for a small sum as well as be housed nearby for this purpose.

It is assumed that a meeting took place between the Duke and the no-longer-anonymous Samuel Smith Spalding, as records show, between February 1794 and June 1800. A bond was drawn up between the two for £500 plus an annuity of £30. The collection, consisting of 2,534 pieces, was originally housed, as requested by Spalding, in a custom-built gallery close to the town of Woodstock. The majority of the collection was Oriental porcelain, Famille Verte, Blue-and-White and Blue Celeste, as well Blanc de Chine, Japanese Black-and-Gold, and Earthenware. Sadly, the custom gallery did not last for long. By 1846 the 5th Duke had the collection moved to the palace – first to the arcade rooms adjacent to the Indian Room, which he had had painted with a mural depicting a tiger-hunt in a tropical landscape, and subsequently to where they are today, displayed in custom glass cabinets around the perimeter of the Great Hall.

The 3rd Duke was gifted a fine Meissen dinner service in return for a pack of hounds.

previous pages One of a pair of nineteenth-century Famille Verte Buddhist lions (*left*); A pair of Chinese Iman beaker vases and a Japanese ovoid *Kakiemon* jar, c. 1680.

opposite and right One of four cabinets displaying the beautiful Meissen dinner service, too precious and delicate to use, but a fine example of the art of porcelain of the time. Sliced lemons are finely crafted to form tureen lids.

following pages Part of the Powder Blue service, exquisitely decorated with Japanese scenes. Blanc de Chine White porcelain from the time of the Kangxi Emperor (1661–1722). These pieces form part of the unique Spalding collection.

FU-KIEN
BLANC-DE-CHINE

Plate XXXII.

Dome Bed.

Mr Ince inv.^t et del.

Darly sculp.

Furniture

The 4th Duke was in a fortunate position to have been left a large inheritance, allowing him to indulge in enhancing the house with lavish decoration and commissioning a gargantuan transformation of the marshy Glyme Valley, which finally allowed the grand bridge to come into its own. His close relationship with George III gave him access to the finest craftsmen and influencers of the time, and the Duke sought the expertise of Sir William Chambers, the designer of Somerset House, to add lustre to the staterooms in the fashionable French style.

THE STATE BED

One of William Chambers' tasks was to design a state bed for the State Bedchamber, which in 1773 was undergoing refurbishment to provide suitably impressive quarters for any royalty that should choose to stay. The design was executed by the established royal cabinetmakers Ince and Mayhew. The Duke, with his knowledge and love of the arts and sciences, became a loyal patron for many years, enjoying a relationship based on a mutual love of fine craftsmanship and superb design.

The bed, which stood over fifteen feet tall (four-and-a-half metres), with a domed canopy supported on carved and gilded fluted bedposts with elaborate plumed helmets perched on each corner, had elements of carving influenced by French ornament and military emblems. The dome was surmounted with a ducal coronet carrying the family coat of arms at the head. Records from 1780 show that the original furnishings in the room and on the bed were in a blue-silk damask with a silk fringed border interlaced with gold. Luckily, fragments of the blue silk were found during investigations being carried out for a proposed restoration. When the bed was rehoused to the Godolphin rooms on the second floor in 1884, it was reupholstered in a coral-pink velvet and point lace *appliqué*, some of which remains, but in poor condition.

While the surviving documents are not precise, it appears that the original design came from Mayhew, with influence and alterations suggested by Chambers and perhaps a considerable amount of involvement from the Duke and Duchess themselves. The end result is a mélange of French Rococo and Neoclassical with a touch of Gothic Revival embellishment that creates a striking focal point for any room.

It is one of my great ambitions to have the bed professionally restored to its former blue-silk glory and housed either in the Third Stateroom, for which it was originally intended, or back in the Godolphin Rooms above the Saloon, which are much in need of bringing back to life.

opposite An engraving of a bed from Ince and Mayhew's *Universal System of Household Furniture*, which is similar in design to the one they made for the state bedroom.

left One of the few known images of the State Bed shown in the Godolphin suite of rooms that are above the south staterooms. It was originally made for the ground floor staterooms and barely fits in the room upstairs. It is missing the original Ducal Crown that sat above the dome.

following pages The Third Stateroom displays an outstanding collection of Boulle furniture by French cabinetmaker André-Charles Boulle, who perfected the technique of inlaying delicate brass work into tortoiseshell.

above and opposite Details of Boulle's incredible craftsmanship.

opposite and right Carved-and-gilded side and console tables were essential pieces of eighteenth-century furniture, often designed by the architect to fit in a specific location along with a complementary mirror above to help reflect the daylight or candlelight. In most of the staterooms at Blenheim they sit between a pair of windows and the marble tops offer a practical surface for displaying objects.

Stiff Leadbetter and Charles Arbuckle were the prominent architects and furnishers to Charles, the 3rd Duke, both at his main home, Langley, and subsequently Marlborough House in London. The 3rd Duke's residency at Blenheim was short lived, mainly because he favoured Langley, but also because his grandmother, Sarah, placed restrictions on his spending and ability to move possessions around, which inhibited his ability to do much. Fortunately, he and his wife seemed content to live at Blenheim without making significant changes, and his main legacy was the building of bookcases in the Long Library to house the Sunderland Collection.

George, the 4th Duke, favoured William Chambers, an artist, architect, and founder-member of the Royal Academy, commissioning him to carry out significant works both in London and at the Blenheim estate. George's first commission working with Chambers was for the Town Hall in Woodstock in 1766, an elegant Neoclassical-style building that is still very much part of the local community today. He then moved on to adding an additional attic floor to Marlborough House in London before turning his attention to Blenheim. Both Marlborough and

Chambers worked closely with Ince and Mayhew as well as continuing to use his other trusted craftspeople to ensure he had control over every detail.

The original furnishings for the State bedroom included a settee, six gilt armchairs, two window seats and two carved gilt curtain cornices; and, as was typical of the mid-eighteenth century, all the furnishings were upholstered in the same cloth, in this case a blue-silk damask. Between the windows was a carved gilt table surmounted with a large gilt pier glass and to one side of the bed a commode probably made in a design from Chambers.

Chambers continued to transform just about every room on the south and east façades, commissioning furniture and decoration from his trusted craftsmen such as Robert Ansell, Thomas Stephens, Sefferin Alken, and Benjamin Thacker to name a few. As lifestyles quickly evolved, so the use of each room was also subject to change, resulting in furnishings specifically made for one area soon becoming obsolete and thus moved to another house or refashioned for another room.

Records from the Steward's daybook and the Ince and Mayhew registers show that work continued up

Suites of furniture, designed by the cabinet makers of the time, were produced for the look and not for comfort.

until around 1797, so over a period of almost twenty-five years Chambers and his protégés, including Ince and Mayhew, had a considerable influence on the furnishings and interior decorating trends of the time.

With around 250 years having passed and eight more dukes, sadly there is little that survives in terms of original furnishings, but in my view that is quite acceptable: rooms should evolve and embrace not only current lifestyles but accept the use of sustainable materials and innovative technologies.

opposite A detail of one of a suite of twelve mahogany side chairs by Mayhew and Ince, c. 1792, showing the ducal coronet and a griffin's head, which is part of the Spencer family crest.

above A recently restored *Directoire bergère* chair, c. 1795, stamped G. Jacob.

Forms of upholstery go as far back as the fourteenth century, when The Worshipful Company of Upholders was formed. (Upholder being the old word for "upholsterer," seemingly derived from tent-making.) Inevitably, it was only the wealthy who could afford the luxury of padded chairs, which became popular in the seventeenth century. Upholders would be responsible for all forms of furnishings and often worked with skilled cabinetmakers who produced the frames.

Original upholstery used a stuffing of sawdust, plant material or animal hair, and it was only during and after the Industrial Revolution (1760–1850) that the textile trade flourished. Modern techniques were developed with skills and techniques that were then passed down through generations.

During the eighteenth century there were some very lavish upholstered pieces at Blenheim, largely forming suites of furniture designed by the era's cabinetmakers like Ince and Mayhew. But these pieces were still mostly produced for looks, not so much for comfort, and were typically placed around the edges of a room and then pulled into place to accommodate larger gatherings as required.

In the last half of the nineteenth century, during the 7th Duke's era, the trend for opulence and comfort when entertaining at home led to a rise in the demand for overstuffed, deep-buttoned large sofas and chairs. Mass-production techniques and better-quality steel-coil springs allowed layers of wadding and cushioning to be built up using lashing cord to hold the springs in place and to ensure they returned to the original position and shape when not being used. This not only created much more comfortable seats but also allowed for the use of elaborate trimmings like deep-bullion fringes, tufted buttoning and brushed fringes. Also, piping cords around seats, arms, and cushions, which were typically upholstered in heavy linens, silk or velvets, added to the overall exotic look.

These traditional upholstery techniques are still very much in use today with most natural materials, like animal hair, having been replaced with some type of foam. Many of the old four-poster bed mattresses at Blenheim were made from horsehair and, inevitably, had lost their shape after many years of use. Thankfully, today we have replaced all the old mattresses with sumptuous new ones, ensuring comfort and sweet dreams even if ensuite bathrooms are in short supply.

previous pages Detail of the intricate gilt-metal lock on a Vermillion japanned cabinet, c.1690. This is one of a near pair and sits in the main corridor on the private East Wing.

left A carved giltwood mini-bergère with a round padded back upholstered in a green damask.

opposite One of a pair of giltwood banquettes upholstered in red damask. The corner seat was reserved for a chaperone.

EARL OF STRAFFORD and
SIR PHILIP MAINWARING

EARL OF STRAFFORD
VAN DYCK

FOUR-POSTER BEDS

An elaborate four-poster was a status symbol in early country houses, but the curtains and canopy, providing privacy and protection from draughts, were also considered somewhat of a necessity. These antique beds are quite impractical today, as the frames are generally too small to accommodate a decent thick, sprung mattress. Because they were originally built for smaller people and to accommodate thin, horsehair mattresses, many original beds have been altered to make them wider and longer. At Blenheim, we don't have an abundance of grand four-poster beds, largely because the second floor, where all the guest bedrooms are situated – with the exception of the Corner Tower Bedroom and the Sunderland Bedroom – has low ceilings.

Lack of available funds has prevented us from restoring the fabric hangings, a job well overdue, as many of the original silk ones have frayed and faded beyond repair. In the Sunderland Bedroom, for example, the colours just don't work with the rug and tapestries, so this becomes one more project added to an already long wish list.

opposite A George III mahogany tester bed with a giltwood cornice carved with scrolls and gadroons. The bed curtains are much in need of replacing and on a long list of restoration work to be carried out when funds permit.

above A nineteenth-century, japanned four-poster tester bed that was fashionable in Europe in the eighteenth and nineteenth centuries. This is in the Tower Bedroom on the south-east corner.

FABRICS AND CURTAINS

In the eighteenth and for much of the nineteenth century, grand staterooms had the walls battened and covered in fabric that matched the curtains and the upholstery. That was the look. Very few of these original fabrics remain. The main fabrics used were silk damask, *brocatelle* or silk velvet, and originally they were only woven to a width of twenty-one inches – not really ideal for walls because it required too many seams. Looms today mostly weave to a more standard width of forty-eight inches, but some of the early traditional designs are still only available at the narrower width.

At Blenheim, the fabrics in the staterooms were installed by the 9th Duke and Consuelo. She sourced in Paris from the best mills, and the installation would have been carried out partially by British craftsmen but also by specialists from the French fabric houses who specialised in luxurious trimmings, which were custom woven to complement their fabrics and often cost more than the fabric itself.

Overlooking the Italian Gardens, this guest bedroom is one of the more modest ones. The furnishings are typical of the French style, with walls and soft furnishings in complementary designs. In this case, the carved cornice of the bed has been covered in fabric, but underneath it would be mahogany matching the bedposts.

left Details of the curtains in the Grand Cabinet, which are in a rich marine blue velvet with a complementary silk tassel fringe. These windows previously had carved gilded pelmets.

opposite Details of curtains in the Bow Window Room, our private dining room. These curtains were replaced by my company around twenty years ago, in time for a visit by Philip, the Duke of Edinburgh, for the Game Fair.

following pages The genius of Capability Brown seen in all its painterly glory: romantic sweeps of grass, a limpid lake now making sense of Vanbrugh's statement bridge, and artfully placed clumps of trees creating vistas and tantalising glimpses of unfolding landscapes.

CHAPTER FOUR

PARK & GARDENS

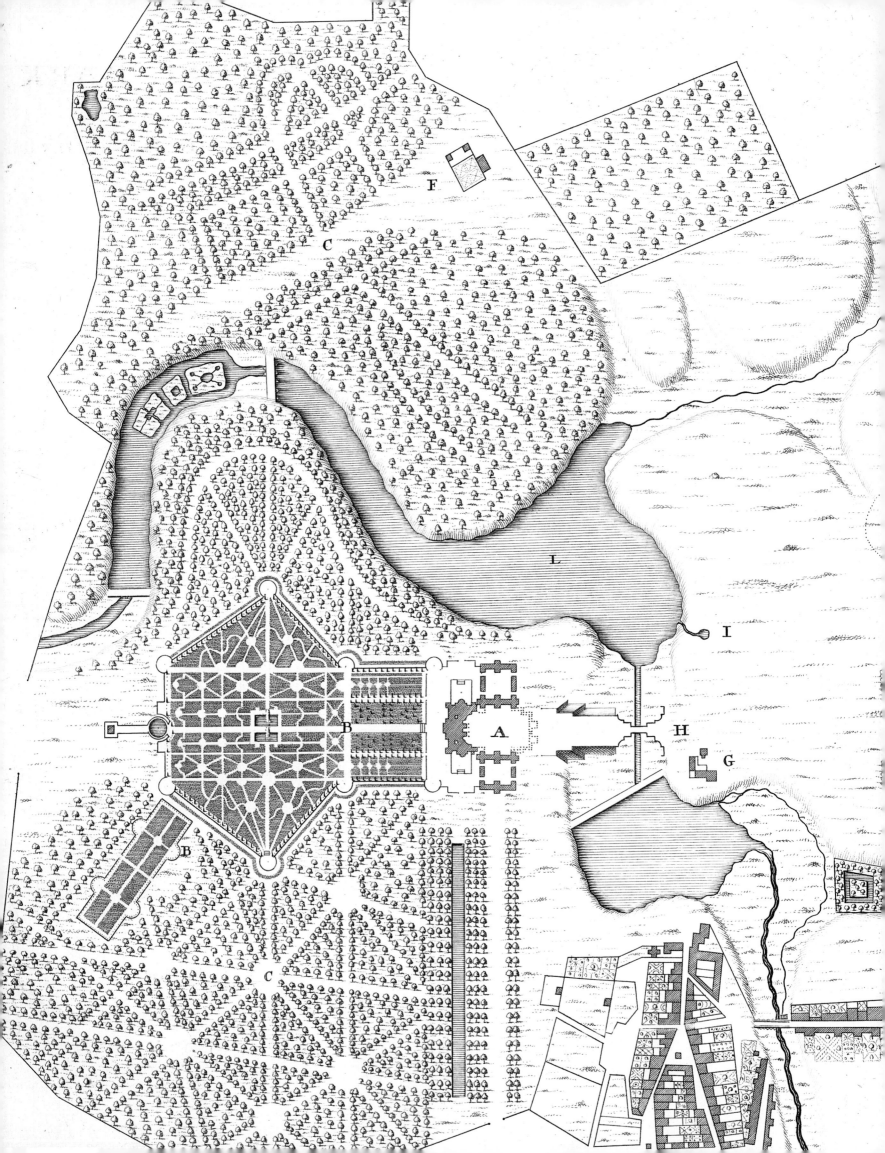

PARK & GARDENS

Woodstock Manor and its extensive parklands was the site gifted to John Churchill by Queen Anne for the building of Blenheim. It was a royal park, renowned for its peerless wooded hunting grounds, although the manor itself was an uninhabited ruin and the surrounding parkland decidedly swampy.

The manor had a romantic history. It was built as a hunting lodge way back in the twelfth century, then extended to become a Royal Palace under Henry II. The palace and its hunting grounds suited King Henry well. He spent much time there with his mistress, the legendary fair Rosamond, reputed to be the most beautiful woman in the kingdom, much to the chagrin of his Queen, Eleanor. Tales were told of a labyrinth of tunnels under Woodstock Park where the lovers would meet, or, conversely, where the jealous Queen stabbed her rival to death, or perhaps both. This doomed romance has been celebrated in folksong, verse, opera, theatrical performance, and a clutch of bodice-ripper novels. What remained of the labyrinth, known as Rosamond's Bower, was demolished when Blenheim was built; but, a paved spring, Fair Rosamond's Well, on the western side of the Great Lake, keeps her memory alive to this day.

Because Blenheim is a monument built by the nation to honour a great military leader, the park and gardens have always been open to the public, which has made finding a quiet, private place for the family living there, a big issue.

Vanbrugh's Vision

That the architect of Blenheim had a background in the theatre comes as no surprise. Vanbrugh chose to site his new, massive seven-acre palace on a raised plateau to the south of the park. He envisaged the approach to his masterpiece, built to be viewed from afar, cutting a swathe through the swampy valley where Woodstock Manor was situated over "the finest bridge in Europe." And as both Vanbrugh and the Duke wanted the palace and the gardens to be finished at the same time, there was feverish activity in every corner of the park. Henry Wise, the Queen's gardener, worked with Vanbrugh to create an ordered, formal background to the mighty palace, while retaining the hunting grounds and ancient

woodlands to the north. A great avenue of elms was created to lead the visitor and the eye towards the palace, and Vanbrugh's finest bridge, which at the time of its creation spanned a narrow canal and a trickle of the river Glyme.

A walled seventy-acre Military Garden was created on the south side where the staterooms looked out over ordered planting. We had only seen plans for this garden in the archives until the drought of 2018 when aerial drone images of the parched South Lawn gave up details of this ancient planting. It was extraordinary to see.

On a more practical level, Henry Wise's seven-acre kitchen garden with fourteen-foot-high (4.2-metre) walls, including a heated section for growing vines, survived

Capability Brown's sweeping changes in the 1770s and exists today, still providing the family and the estate with cutting flowers, fruit, and vegetables.

The landscaping of the park was always about vistas and focal points. Subsequent landscapers and gardeners have interpreted the park in different ways—moving mountains of earth, building temples, altering water courses—but they all had the same objective: vistas and focal points. Some of my forebears wished to temper the vision with colourful patches of flowers and shrubs and patterned parterres. The big challenge today is to incorporate all these differing visions and personalities into a cohesive whole.

previous pages The original garden design by Henry Wise overseen, of course, by Vanbrugh. The great parterre—with it clipped plants trained into precise geometric forms and regimented ornamental woods and topiary gardens—would all be swept away by Capability Brown.

above The main approach from the north to Blenheim Palace. In Vanbrugh's original plan, this drive would take the awe-inspired visitor all the way from Ditchley Gate, straight along the impressive Grand Avenue, and over his famous bridge, the eye drawn to a view of the finest of palaces set on a slight rise, a journey of about two-and-a-half miles.

opposite Thanks to its heritage as a forested deer park, Blenheim is home to the greatest number of ancient oaks in Europe, many of them over 900 years old. Our forestry team have propagated more than 3000 seedlings from these ancient oaks to ensure that the legacy lives on.

above Life isn't just about vistas; even in a palace you have to live and you have to eat. This is a view toward the walled kitchen garden, where cutting flowers and vegetables help to fill the house and the larders.

The Grand Avenue

Along the one-and-a-half-mile length of the Grand Avenue, double ranks of elms were planted on either side in 1707, but it was a grand design that never really took off, as many of the elms struggled to survive and the result was a bit patchy. The elms were replanted between 1896 and 1902 with nearly 2,500 trees, but then along came Dutch Elm Disease, and in the 1970s my father had the elms finally grubbed out and replaced with lime trees, which have flourished.

The Grand Avenue was envisaged as a dramatic approach to the palace. A good long gallop from the Ditchley Gate and a setting for the Column of Victory. Perhaps not a full-tilt gallop, though, as at various times fences, gates, and cattlegrids have been installed and removed in order to contain sheep and cattle. The 9th Duke, envisaging reckless motorists carving up the avenue, had a huge block of stone embedded right in the middle, which thankfully has since been removed. The main entrance, The Mall, is through the East Court and just a short drive up from Woodstock. It, too, was planted with elms, eventually replaced by plane trees and limes.

The park is a busy, working estate as it has always been, and now it is dedicated to the sustainable management of woodlands and the raising of happy, healthy livestock.

above The sheep are a pedigree native breed requiring less veterinary intervention than most.

opposite The column of victory, built in 1727, five years after John Churchill died, is 134-feet-high. The statue atop the column, showing the victorious Duke in Roman military garb, was sculpted by Sir Henry Cheere.

The Finest Bridge in Europe

It is a very grand structure, likened by some to the Rialto Bridge in Venice. Bit difficult to imagine, but Vanbrugh's original plans for the bridge included a colonnaded superstructure. Personally, I am grateful those plans were shelved as, in its present form, it blends harmoniously into Capability Brown's landscape. When you see it now, built from the same mellow stone as the palace, it is difficult to imagine one without the other; however, 1st Duchess Sarah was scathing about this bridge, deeming it an unnecessary expense and far too grandiose a structure to span the trickle of river that flowed beneath it at that time.

The bridge was designed as a "habitable viaduct", and the big surprise is that there are secret passageways and thirty-three windowless rooms within the structure, some with fireplaces and chimneys, and one room so big it could have been a ballroom. Who intended to live in the bridge? That has never been established. When Capability Brown redesigned the landscape of the park and created the great lake that finally made sense of the proportions of the bridge, those rooms were submerged, and it is only now, as the dredging of the lake and repairs to the bridge take place, that many of these rooms have come to light. Some have plasterwork, and there is evidence of a working kitchen. Curiouser and curiouser.

left and following pages Bridge and palace coexist in perfect harmony. The bridge, described by a contemporary gardening "expert" as a "monstrous bridge over a vast hollow" has a central arch 100 feet wide, flanked by smaller arches and four corner towers. It did indeed span a "vast hollow" back then. Before the lake, the bridge extended over a body of water that could best be described as a canal with steep banks. Sir Sacheverell Sitwell, brother to Dame Edith and Sir Osbert, was a distinguished twentieth-century writer on Baroque architecture. His opinion of the lake? "The lake at Blenheim is the one great argument of the landscape gardener. There is nothing finer in Europe."

Painting with Landscape

Times change and tastes change, and so the formality of the parterres favoured by Vanbrugh and Henry Wise were looking tired and old-fashioned, thought George, the 4th Duke, who now had the money to do something about it. It was the 1760s and at that time there was one landscape architect whose reputation towered above all others: Lancelot "Capability" Brown. Brown's big idea was to brush aside the regimented and the symmetrical and replace the geometric artificiality of the Baroque with a sweep of nature—but nature ably assisted by man of course. He started work at Blenheim in 1764 and worked there on and off for the next ten years. His vision for Blenheim, as indeed it was for many of the finest estates in Britain, was to paint a vast romantic picture using water, grass, trees, and artful "ruins."

Architect William Chambers, who added a touch of eighteenth-century elegance to the interior architecture, was responsible for artful additions to Brown's romantic landscape, in particular the Bladon Bridge, the Temple of Diana, and a Palladian gateway on the west wall of the walled garden.

Brown's big idea was to brush aside the regimented and the symmetrical and replace the geometric artificiality of the Baroque with a sweep of nature, nature ably assisted by man, of course.

opposite above Capability Brown also built structures, like Bladon Bridge, but his creations were designed to sit within his romantic landscapes.

above Brown's collaborator, the architect William Chambers, built follies, romantic ruins, and temples to enhance Brown's landscapes. The Temple of Diana, sketched here by John Yenn, is one such building at Blenheim. It is delightfully situated near the lake, providing a classical focal point for the eye and a place to pause and refresh the soul. See it in its natural setting on page 252.

The Great Lake

The creation of this tree-lined lake was Capability Brown's true stroke of genius. To create the lake, he dammed the river Glyme, creating as he did so the Grand Cascades, adding sounds and sparkles. Creating the forty-acre lake was a complicated affair that required a very substantial dam, a lot of earth-moving and blind faith in Vanbrugh's bridge being strong enough to withstand the considerable inrush of water. It was worth all the effort, careful planning and expense. The lake is a magical addition to the park; it can be seen or glimpsed from so many viewpoints, and it has developed a flora and fauna all its own.

Having a lake in your park carries a big responsibility to ensure that fish, waterbirds and plantings are all happy. The lake needs to be at least two metres deep to support aquatic life, but in recent times the build-up of silt left it only twenty to thirty centimetres deep. We have just completed a two-year programme to remove the silt on the Queen Pool side and the result is spectacular, with even the otters enjoying the new refined water. Back in the 1890s the 9th Duke faced the same silt problem. It is said that when he finally sealed his marriage to American heiress Consuelo, he immediately telegrammed home, not so say he was the happiest man alive, but with the instructions: "Now dredge the lake!"

The boathouse, tucked into the shelter of the lakeshore, was built at the instigation of Lilian Hammersley, the 8th Duke's second Duchess, for private family use, and subsequent generations have had much fun there. We learned to sail and water-ski on that lake, and enjoyed many family barbeques and parties in and around the boathouse when the park was closed to visitors. It has also been used for the barefoot waterskiing championships, now an annual event as part of the Blenheim Triathlon.

opposite A glorious clump of trees in many colours reflected in the lake. Although these are not necessarily trees planted by Capability Brown, subsequent planting has followed and enhanced his ideas for stands of trees that fit into an overall composition.

below The boathouse built by the 8th Duke's second wife, Lilian Hammersley, so the family could have some fun on the lake. It's a popular venue now for boating, parties and events. Winston Churchill painted it; and at Christmas it gets all dressed up.

Trees and Grass

To create the perfect view for visitors driving or riding in the park, Brown planted trees judiciously – to both hide and reveal – offering tantalising glimpses that made people want to explore further. He planted four stands of beech trees on either side of the bridge and massed cedars, acacias, poplar trees, chestnuts and beech around the cascades. The 3rd Duke had begun to plant trees around the perimeter of the estate, and Brown ran with the plan, planting double rows of trees that hint at the presence of a vast forest beyond. Throughout the park, he placed trees with a painterly eye for composition, planting clumps for impact here and single specimens there to draw the eye, never forgetting the colours, shapes and heights of foliage year-round to surprise and delight.

About 150 years later, the 9th Duke planted nearly half a million new trees, using them to create and frame views, just as Brown had done but not always where Brown had put them. These plantings created a more densely wooded scene than Brown's original scheme. The 9th Duke's most notable clumps are on the east side of the river and on the high ground of the northern park.

Brown obliterated what remained of Henry Wise's formal Military Garden to the south, creating the rolling South Lawn that runs from the palace to as far as the eye can see. This is separated from the park proper by a ha-ha, or sunken fence, to keep livestock away from the house, while opening up views across to Bladon Village and St. Martin's Church. He also removed the formal stone terraces in the Great Court, replacing the cobbles with an oval lawn surrounded by a gravel carriage drive. It was a very different look.

previous pages and left The quiet, peaceful landscaped lake was formed by damming the river Glyme, and the consequent cascades are both beautiful and powerful. The area above the cascade is a rock garden. The story goes that while the 9th Duke was busy building the water terraces, Duchess Gladys, feeling ignored and bored, fashioned her revenge rock garden with the help of a strong gardener's boy, planting it with saxifrage and yellow primulas.

above Through the trees, a glimpse of the Woodstock Gate, or the Arch of Triumph, built by Hawksmoor in 1723. Hawksmoor based it on the Arch of Titus, constructed on the Via Sacra in Rome in AD 81. From here you get a spectacular first glimpse of the lake and Grand Bridge.

right Hensington Gate, with its two Hawksmoor pillars, is a Capability Brown construction designed to be the new main entrance, making logical sense of the approach to the palace. Capability Brown's total bill for works at Blenheim, never mind the labour and materials, was £16,000, or nearly £2.5 million today.

Entrances and Exits

This is a story of first impressions. Blenheim was lucky to have two masters of the art of inspiring awe in the visitor, and even in family, friends and staff habituated to the sights. During Vanbrugh's time, the main entrance to Blenheim Park was from Woodstock, in a direct line to the grand gate of the East Court leading into the Great Court. The entrance from Bladon to the south of the park was only a stile in his time, and at the northern end, the Ditchley Gate at the conclusion of the Grand Avenue was little more than a hole in the wall. Hawksmoor came up with some splendid designs for a Ditchley Gate, but it was never going to be a practical main entrance as it was so far from the palace, and, one could say, a little too obvious – no hazard or surprise.

Then along came the second hero, Capability Brown, whose sweeping changes included designing two different carriage drives into Blenheim Park. He improved the entrance from Woodstock with an elm-lined mall, moving two gate piers designed by Hawksmoor from the east of the garden to become Hensington Gate. That main entrance works on every level as the palace, lake and bridge come progressively into view across the valley. His next stroke of genius was to create a drive from the Bladon Gate. This southern approach is longer and more picturesque than the direct line from Woodstock, cleverly making capital of changes in the level of the land so that the lake and river can be glimpsed through the trees. A late eighteenth-century guidebook describes the drive: "The water, the Palace, the Gardens, the Great Bridge, the Pillar, Woodstock, and other near and remote objects, open and shut upon the eye like enchantment." Job done.

Grand Plans and Passions

With the enchanting landscape of Blenheim Park now so pleasingly crafted by the master, it fell to subsequent heirs to maintain and improve their legacy and enjoy the freedom to express themselves with their various projects. George, the 5th Duke, had grown up with Lancelot Brown and his father moving trees and earth and water to create the idyllic scene that lay before him on his succession. George was no fool: he was a bibliophile and a botanist to professional standards, but he was a weak character and a spendthrift who caused a huge blip in the fortunes of the estate. However, he was passionate about plants and astute enough to create his new gardens well to the west of the estate. He set about ordering thousands of plants from far flung exotic places that he planted in themed and landscaped gardens and grottos. He fashioned a Chinese garden, aviaries, a melon house, fountains, rock gardens and streams, unfortunately at the expense of looking after the "bones" of the park: the lake, the dam, and the cascade. His intention was to create the finest botanical and flower gardens in Europe, and while he was criticised for trans-forming "the rich draperies of Brown's design" into a "harlequin jacket of little clumps and beds," his rock garden and his arboretum blended in seamlessly. Attempts were made in the nineteenth century to preserve some of George's private gardens, but finally the kangaroo and emu enclosure, the Eskimo hut and his various pavilions were demolished and now only a few exotic trees survive.

A Touch of Versailles

previous pages and above The Great Court to the front of the palace faces the north and the Column of Victory. It was grassed over by Capability Brown to fit in with his romantic parkland theme, but the 9th Duke wanted change and commissioned Achille Duchêne to reinstate a formal courtyard. According to Consuelo's memoirs, "Vanbrugh had contemplated the forecourt Duchêne designed as we discovered when breaking through foundations. It was very simple, re-introducing large simple gravel and paving to echo the original design which can be seen in 18th C engravings."

left The Chateau of Versailles, built in the late seventeenth century, was the inspiration behind the work of French garden designer Achille Duchêne, commissioned by the 9th Duke to restore formality and order to a park that had been sorely neglected for decades.

To improve Blenheim and bring it up to date, the 9th Duke married money. Ironically, considering Blenheim was a gift from a grateful nation for squashing French ambitions in Europe, he turned to a Frenchman, Achille Duchêne. Although Duchêne had worked a lot in Britain, his grounding was in the grand tradition of the formal parterres and plantings of André Le Nôtre, whose vision was responsible for the gardens at Versailles.

Duchêne started work on Capability Brown's simple, grassy courtyard. Romantic it may have been, but it was not, the 9th Duke believed, a suitable setting for a grand palace. The grass and carriage drive were removed, and the Great Court was refashioned more or less to Vanbrugh's original formal design, which, obviously not wanting to be obliterated, was still traceable under the layers of grass and gravel.

The beautiful symmetry is perfectly viewed from above at the windows of our family dining room.

The Italian Garden

Many attempts had been made over the centuries to establish some sort of private family garden to the east in the area bordered by the private apartments and the orangery overlooked by the family dining room. The 1st Duchess had a flower garden there, but by the time the 9th Duke succeeded it was an overwrought late-Victorian sunken area with nothing much to recommend it.

Between 1908 and 1910, the garden was entirely redesigned by Duchêne. He created a grand parterre using dwarf box to make an intricate but crisp pattern infilled with gravel, with paths of crushed brick and accents of topiary centred around a gilded fountain made by the American sculptor Thomas Waldo Story. Scouring the undercroft and other parts of the park, Duchêne found Italian bronze sculptures dating from around 1700 by the Florentine sculptor Massimiliano Soldani, which were gifts to the 1st Duke. These he mounted on limestone pedestals in the corners. The garden is totally symmetrical and kept in perfect shape with constant care and pruning, recalling the meticulous gardens surrounding Italian Renaissance palaces. The beautiful symmetry is perfectly viewed from above, from where the garden delivers a constant delight to the eye from the windows of our family dining room.

Supposedly the family's private garden, but, in reality, it isn't, and visitors can enjoy the intricate box and yew topiary. The joyful mermaid fountain, recently cleaned and re-gilded, is by the American sculptor Thomas Waldo Story.

Water Terraces

By 1925 the Duke had restored much of the palace's formal setting to the north and east, and he turned his attention to the surviving Victorian garden to the west. The site was difficult, sloping away gently from the house and then falling steeply towards the lake. The Duke and Duchêne were both determined to "make a liaison between the façade of Vanbrugh and the water line of the lake made by Brown." The Duke argued:

> to reconcile these conflicting ideas is difficult. The difficulty is not diminished when you remember that the façade of the house is limited and the line of the lake is limitless. As an example, if you turn your back to the lake and look at the façade your parterre, basin etc is in scale to the façade, but if you look at the same parterre from the rotunda to the lake it is out of scale with the panorama.

To address the slope problem, the site was terraced to create two distinct levels, reminiscent of the Parterre d'Eau at Versailles. Duchêne wanted to emulate Versailles with running water and spouting fountains, but the Duke preferred the "limpidity" of still water in the more subdued Italian style. He wrote to Duchêne that,

> limpidity of water is pleasing and possesses a romance. You have got this effect in the basins and in the large area of water contained by the Lake. Be careful not to destroy this major emotion which Nature has granted you for the sake of what may possibly be a vulgar display of waterworks which can be seen at any exhibition or public park. Turn all these matters over in your mind when you are at rest in the evening, for it is only by thought, constant thought and mature reflection that artists have left their great works for the enjoyment of posterity.

right The Upper Water Terrace on the west side overlooks the sunken main section of the gardens. Parterre beds of box and coloured gravel are bordered with limestone kerb walls.

following pages Where the lower water terrace meets the lake. The Bernini fountain was probably a model for the one that stands in Rome's Piazza Navona. The four figures arranged on a rocky plinth surrounding the central obelisk depict and the rivers Nile, Ganges, Plata, and Tiber.

The terraces are separated by a retaining wall, held up by a series of pillars, niches and caryatids carved by Jules Edouard Visseaux. The face of one of them, at least, was carved from life – from one of the gardeners.

As well as an artistic challenge that both men obviously took very seriously, the water terraces posed an engineering challenge. The Duke insisted on using Rosamond's Well for the water, which was piped beneath the whole length of the southern lake to the engine house at the cascade and from there back to the palace, leaving the lake limpidly undisturbed.

Duchêne got his fountains and some running water on the drop between the two levels, and the Duke got his calm limpidity at the top.

The terraces needed a focal point. Blenheim Park again provided the answer. Hiding in the shrubbery – what luck! – was a Bernini fountain in marble and limestone that had been gifted to the 1st Duke by the Spanish ambassador to the Papal Court in Rome. The original now takes pride of place on the lower terrace and a copy was created for symmetry. Both are sited in square pools. Urns, pots and statuary complete the picture. Of particular note are a pair of haughty sphinxes, whose faces were modelled on the beautiful Gladys, the 9th Duke's second Duchess.

The Rose Garden

We have John Winston, the 7th Duke, to thank for the Rose Garden. The circular rosary has radiating paths and a central fountain surrounded by symmetrical beds; each bed is filled with a variety of roses. It was laid on the site of his grandfather's former Chinese garden. The surviving rosary was carefully restored by my father.

The garden is home to more than 1,800 roses, chosen mostly for their fragrance, making walking around the garden an unforgettable sensory experience. It is usually in full bloom at the end of June or early in July, but changing weather patterns are making blooming difficult to predict. As everyone who cultivates roses will know, it is a labour-intensive task keeping the garden looking at its best. The garden is contained within a circular walk surrounded by blue catmint and arched over by slender hoops supporting climbing white roses.

The Secret Garden

What is so lovely about this garden is the sheer romance of it. It was created by my very stiff-upper-lipped grandfather, who was accurately described as having "an arrogant stare and bad manners." He did, however, have a good heart, but a gruff bark, and the convincing persona of a formidable, old-school English aristocrat. He quite terrified me as a child, thus my brother and I spent more time outside in the park and gardens than in the house.

opposite and above The glory of the rose garden. The gardeners have calculated that to encourage more flowers they have to deadhead about 12,000 blooms every season.

following pages The romantic riot that is the Secret Garden, one for all seasons, mixing old trees, new planting, winding paths, and water features. Not surprisingly, it is a very popular backdrop for wedding photographs.

Bert, as the 10th Duke was known, had always had
an interest in gardening, but his interest was pragmatic.
At this home Lowesby Hall in Leicestershire, where
he first settled into married life with my grandmother,
Mary Cadogan, he had grown and sold vegetables from
his kitchen garden. When Bert inherited Blenheim he
brought his gardener, Tom Page, from Lowesby. Tom
set about establishing greenhouses, vegetable plots, fruit
orchards and beds of cutting flowers for the house. But
Bert was about to unleash a secret passion: in 1954 he
conceived a plan for a three-acre, wild, Italian-style
garden with pools, pathways, rocks, water courses
and freestyle planting. This project filled his life with
purpose and energy and brought a new dimension
to the formal sweeping landscapes and parterres that
had always defined the park at Blenheim. Bert's secret
garden is hardly a secret any more, as the gardens
at Blenheim are open to visitors year-round, and, of
course, the garden has been extensively renovated and
replanted – but Bert's well-hidden wild romantic side is
still in evidence here. It is very touching.

The Roundel

Situated en route from the south side of the house
to the Kitchen Garden is a delightful sculpture of
cascading cherubs set in an ornamental pond that was
restored by my father in 2012 with generous support
from our US Blenheim Foundation. As a child I never
noticed this much, as nearby is a more natural pond,
suitably hidden from onlookers, where we could ice
skate if the winters were harsh enough. The present
water jets supply a forceful yet strategic "halo" over the
cherubs, enhancing the subject without distracting
from them.

Before the round pond, the cherubs, which used to
ornament the upper arches of the Great Hall, sat upon a
"roundabout" of yew and box hedging. It was the 10th Duke
who moved them to the garden and my father who gave
them their pond.

The Churchill Garden

It was my always father's wish to create a garden to celebrate the connection between his cousin and godfather, Sir Winston Churchill, and Blenheim Palace, where Winston was born and where he spent so much pleasurable and creative time. There is now a trail through the formal gardens to the memorial garden, which was opened a year after my father's death in June 2015 by Her Royal Highness the Duchess of Cornwall, who is now, of course, our Queen Camilla.

The Temple of Diana is the centrepiece. It was designed by Sir William Chambers as part of Capability Brown's revamp of Blenheim Park in the early 1770s. It is now better known as the spot where Winston nervously proposed to Clementine Hozier while sheltering from the rain after a stroll around the rose garden. It is undoubtedly a romantic spot with views across Capability Brown's lake. It worked its magic on Clementine, and they were married a year later. The garden has a 295-foot (ninety-metre) granite path representing a timeline of Churchill's ninety-year life, winding through seasonal beds of magnolias, poppies, cornflowers, crocuses, and lilac.

An impressive bust of Churchill in his wartime boiler suit is positioned on a stone plinth overlooking the lake. The sculptor, Oscar Nemon, was a friend of Winston's and varied sculptures of his favourite subject are to be found all over the world from the lobby of the House of Commons to Bletchley Park, New York, Copenhagen, Moscow, and Canberra to name but a few. The two men first met in Marrakesh in 1951. Nemon had lost almost all his family to the Holocaust, and he viewed Churchill with a depth of feeling which is powerfully evident in these forceful portraits.

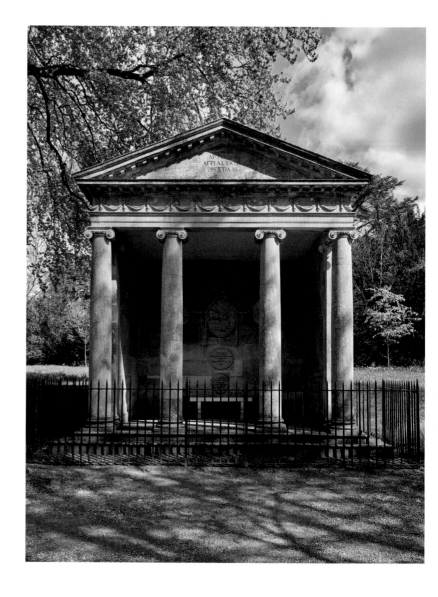

above right A young Winston Churchill and his Clementine photographed to mark their engagement in 1908.

right The Temple of Diana, designed by William Chambers as part of Capability Brown's romantic landscaping. It is a perfect backdrop for a proposal.

opposite The sculptor Oscar Nemon recorded finding his friend and subject "bellicose, challenging, and deliberately provocative." Nemon was himself the subject of Churchill's only sculpture, created while Nemon worked.

CHURCHILL

1874 — 1965

A Living Artwork

The hedge maze within the walled garden at Blenheim is created from more than 3,000 individual yew trees. It is two miles in length and is the second largest hedge maze in Britain (out-mazed in size only by Longleat) – but the largest hedge maze to tell a story. The story it tells is of the 1st Duke of Marlborough's military victories, featuring a cannon firing, pyramids of cannon balls, flags, banners, trumpets and the letters BLENHEIM in the centre. You have to stand on one of the bridges in order to really appreciate the design and also to spot the V sign in honour of Winston Churchill. It was commissioned by my father in 1987, but as it took four years for the hedges to grow it wasn't opened to the public until 1991. I remember the excitement surrounding the opening of the maze, and it has remained a popular attraction over the years.

Here's an interesting fact: the polymer £5 note features a green-foil hologram of our maze in honour of Winston Churchill's birthplace.

Inspiration for the design of the maze came from Grinling Gibbons's stone sculptures, the *Panoply of Victory* for the roof of Blenheim Palace. It takes six people with hedge trimmers a week to prune the tapered yew hedges every October. It was designed by Adrian Fisher and Randoll Coate in the mid-1980s.

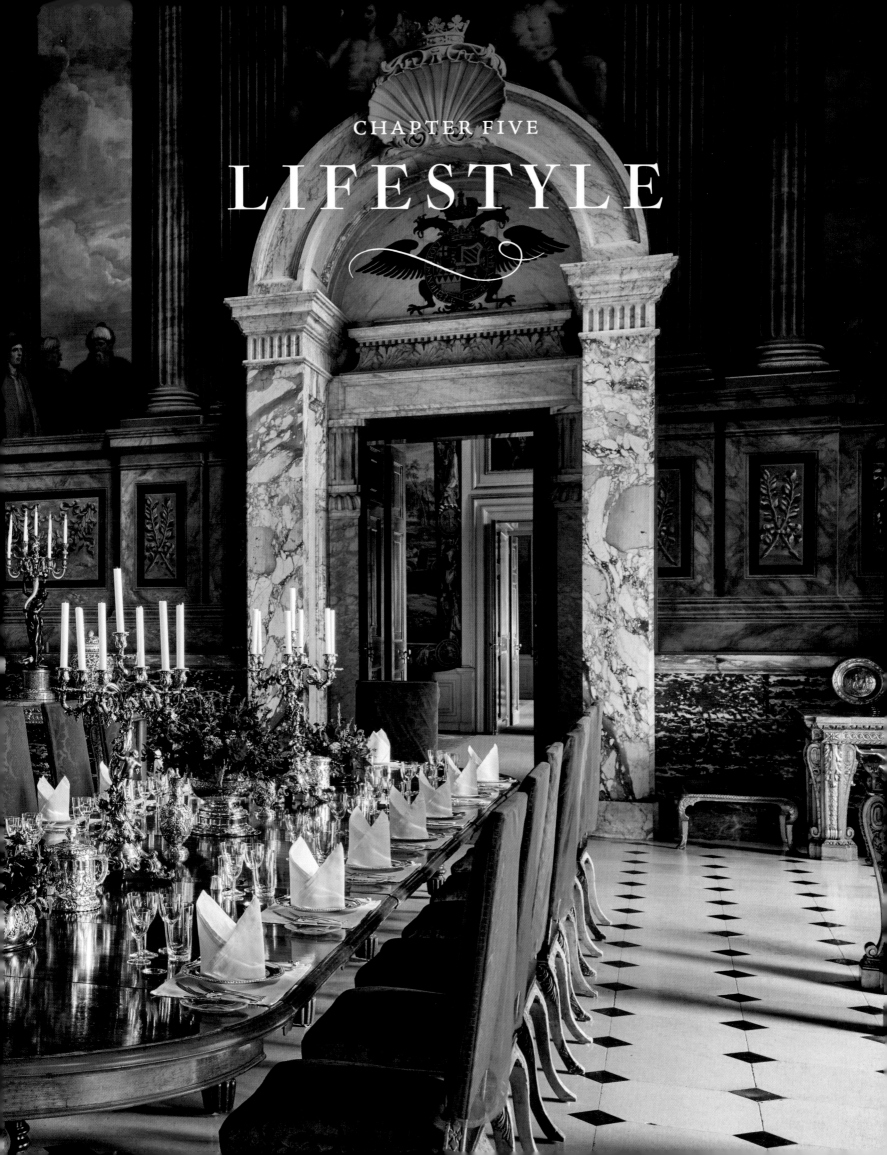

CHAPTER FIVE

LIFESTYLE

LIFESTYLE

In our leisure we reveal what kind of people we are.

OVID, ROMAN POET

Passing time, filling days with meaningful activity when there's no actual work to be done, is one of the principal challenges facing the leisured classes. Many of my ancestors, both men and women, were well-read, well-educated, artistically, politically and strategically savvy, sitting on a wealth of accumulated knowledge that was rarely channelled. Of course, there's the flip side: there were others whose main gifts were for self-indulgence on a grand scale, but fate dictated to them all that apart from ceremonial roles, it was never their destiny to get involved in the world of work. There were staff to dress and undress them; to summon them to table; to put food on their plates; to cook, clean, manage and maintain house, garden and estate; to advise on investments and purchases – in short, there was nothing left for many of them to do other than maintain their position in society and keep up with the fashions and scruples of a changing world. So, this was the challenge: to make a life of leisure both fulfilling and purposeful.

previous pages Table set in the Grand Saloon for a formal dinner. The butler and the underbutler are in charge of laying the table and creating the perfect setting for each occasion.

opposite On very grand occasions, such as a royal visit, the footmen would have worn a special livery in the Marlborough colours with embroidered borders and silver tassels.

Entertaining

Social gatherings, whether formal, casual, sporting or political have always played a large part in the life of Blenheim. Who could ask for a more perfect venue, with its plentiful accommodation, grand staterooms, beautiful park complete with a lake, stables and kennels and a well-staffed household? The only downside, even today, is the lack of bathrooms, especially ensuite bathrooms with power showers. It was not until the arrival of Consuelo Vanderbilt and, subsequently, my grandfather that the inconvenient and dangerous clutter of hot-water jugs, bowls, commodes and hip baths were slowly replaced by plumbing.

THE WAY IT USED TO BE

Large gatherings were often focused on an important event either celebrating a ball, a family wedding or a hunting-and-shooting weekend party, or often a combination of them all. In earlier times this proved much more testing in terms of planning, travelling and, not least, packing. Often five changes of clothes per-day would be commonplace: one for breakfast, one for "taking the air" for ladies, or hunting or shooting for the men. Depending on the venue, the outdoor outfit may suffice for lunch or a picnic on the lawn, but if inside, society's unwritten rules would require another change. Then clean, dry clothes would be required for tea, and then for dinner a final change into formal black or white tie for men and long dress for women. Therefore, for one long weekend stay, and bearing in mind you can't wear the same thing twice, one person would require at least twenty outfits – never mind the jewellery – which meant many hefty trunks loaded into horse-drawn carriages.

To add to the complexities, guests would arrive with their own staff, who also needed to be housed and fed, loading additional pressures on an already busy household and creating the potential for belowstairs scandals and rivalries.

There is a description of the banquet for the thirty-six noble and titled guests for a royal shooting party in 1896 from Gerald Horne, a young hall-boy at the time. It gives one an idea of the effort that all sides went into to stage such a glittering occasion. After this four-day party, Consuelo and the 9th Duke took a much-needed holiday.

I went up and looked down and there it was: all gleaming with wealth. I think the first thing that struck me was the flashing headgear of the ladies. The Blue Hungarian (Band) was playing and there was the Prince himself looking really royal and magnificent in miliary uniform. The table was laid of course with the silver-gilt service, the old silver Duke, (the Garrard centrepiece) busy writing as usual in the very middle of it all, and the royal footmen waiting side by side with our own.

Fortunately, today there is less formality and, of course, modern transportation makes a weekend visit far simpler, more spontaneous and less time-consuming.

THE WAY WE LIVE NOW

There is a beautiful room on the east side of the house (traditionally known as the Bow Window Room) that has always been the venue for family dining. We don't have an informal breakfast room or shooting lunch venue (much needed), so there has always been an air of formality in the room whether for two or twenty-two. If just *en famille*, we would use the same table but reduced to its minimal size; it would sit within the Bow Window with views over the beautiful Italian Gardens. Although lunch or dinner may be three courses and formally served by household staff, a butler and under-butler, the menus would have very much been selected by my father and/or a stepmother and featuring as much seasonal food as possible from our own kitchen garden: home-raised lamb, venison, chicken, eggs and, in the past, beef. I remember well in my grandfather's day having home-churned butter and cream from our own Jersey cows and, perhaps not such a pleasant memory, ox tongue and sweetbreads. But I have always enjoyed the taste of a local game bird, which makes a delicious, economic and healthy meal.

opposite A setting for a shooting tea. There are very few places for an informal meal or where children can eat in the palace. This is one of my favourite spots, tucked at the end of the main corridor on the private side, just outside the pantry and overlooked by a portrait of Consuelo.

To this day I can remember accompanying my father to help pick up the birds and then the aroma of a steak and kidney pie served in front of a roaring fire.

WHAT'S ON THE MENU?

A typical summer lunch menu may be cold pheasants' eggs, home-grown melon or asparagus as a starter; a main course of Coronation chicken and cold cuts served with baby new potatoes, baby vegetables, and salad. For pudding, or dessert, there would be home-grown peaches, grapes, plums, strawberries, raspberries, or any fruit in season, or a fresh homemade sorbet.

An autumnal shooting lunch on the other hand would be quite heart-warming: a lovely beef stew, cottage pie, steak and kidney pudding, maybe a pheasant casserole. In any event it would be typically British pub-like food. For pudding, a crumble, fruit tart, sponge pudding (spotted dick in my grandfather's day), followed by a cheese board and port. It was often difficult to get the men up from their chairs and in the mood to head out again for a couple more drives before coming home for tea.

While my grandfather was alive, I have fond memories of shooting lunches in tenant farmers' houses cooked by their wives – a much simpler and more appropriate way to have a shooting lunch. To this day I can remember accompanying my father to help pick up the birds, and then the aroma of a steak and kidney pie served in front of a roaring fire.

opposite Guests can expect a beautifully presented breakfast tray and a newspaper.

top right A page from the *Household Accounts* book, dated September 1720. This would have been during the brief time the 1st Duke and Duchess were living in the unfinished palace.

right The menu board, so the kitchen and serving staff know what goes with what and in what order.

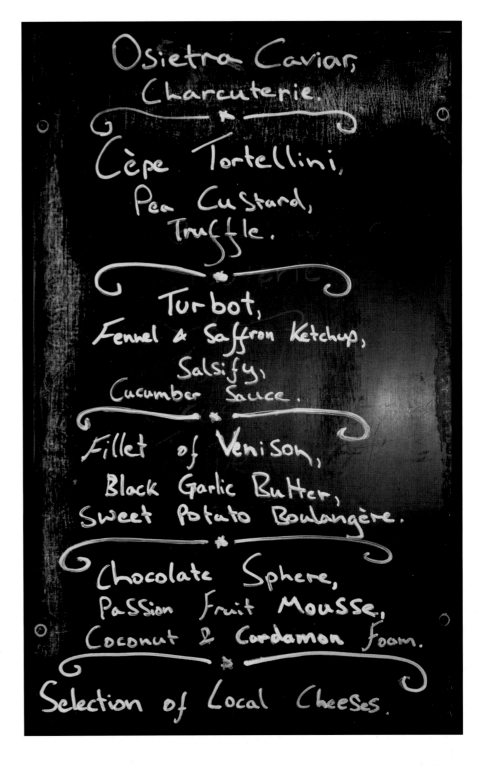

A Family Christmas

Many of my fond memories of entertaining at Blenheim involve special family occasions. Christmas lunch served in the family dining room with lots of cousins and aunts and uncles, following a church service in Woodstock and a brisk walk back to the house. The staff were always initiating or participating in practical jokes targeting one of us. The starter would normally be foie gras *en croûte* or smoked salmon, generously supplied by a family member, followed by a huge turkey carved by my father with all the trimmings. The pudding, of course, was the traditional plum pudding filled with coins and followed by mince pies. The table was always adorned with elegant Christmas crackers, and these were pulled after the pudding with the entire table crossing their arms and tugging after the command had been given. I never seemed to win but nonetheless donned the regulatory paper crown, happily engaging in relaxed conversation until it was time to watch the Queen's Christmas message.

The evening tradition of a formal dinner in the Saloon, as far as I know instigated by my grandfather, would follow. No chance to digest lunch, take a much needed walk, let alone open gifts or indulge in a siesta. As a child I was not allowed to attend the evening dinner until I had reached twelve or thirteen (boarding-school age), but I might have attended the predinner drinks before being whisked away by Nanny for a more modest supper.

Christmas evening was always incredibly special for a youngster. The crowd was mainly family members staying in the house, along with a few close locals who had the stamina to get dressed up and eat yet another large meal. But as I got older and many of my cousins had grown up, moved on, married and had their own family Christmases, the group consisted of my father's close friends or neighbours and we grown-up children who were invited.

Typically, after dinner we would play games: a massive treasure hunt often set up by my half-brother, Edward, and myself or a game of bridge for older members and billiards for the younger. Sadly, none of us are particularly musical, so playing the piano or singing didn't feature much unless we were lucky enough to have a talented guest.

CHRISTMAS 2020
MENU

BORSCH
****
ROAST TURKEY
SAGE & ONION STUFFING
PIGS IN BLANKETS
ROAST POTATOES
SPROUTS WITH BACON & CHESTNUTS
ROAST PARSNIPS
GLAZED CARROTS
****
BROWN BREAD ICECREAM
MORELLO CHERRIES
****
MINCE PIES & BRANDY BUTTER
****
CHOCOLATES

Royal Connections

It's hard to think of a more solid royal connection than that of Queen Anne and the 1st Duke and Duchess of Marlborough. Sarah was her confidante (or more intimate companion as some more salacious sources, such as the film *The Favourite*, would have it), and John was her trusted Commander in Chief and a gifted diplomat who secured England's influence in Europe. The Queen and the Marlboroughs had their disagreements but never lost respect for one another. For this closeness they suffered much abuse from others seeking to undermine their positions. Sarah had her opinions of Anne's successors to the throne, which suggests a continuing closeness with the House of Hanover. She describes the lumpen King George I as:

> *A good natur'd Man … he was not very bright, nor would he have made any great Figure in History. He was satisfied with his pin-money & knowing nothings about laws & English customs, depended on his Ministers for guidance but he would only act lawfully.*

She didn't have much time for Queen Caroline, the wife of George I's son, who had annoyed her when she became the Princess of Wales in 1714 and infuriated her further when she took the throne in 1727. She wrote, again in her private notebook, that Queen Caroline had:

> *Publickly in the Drawing room, before a great deal of Company, said a great many horrid things of the Duke of Marlborough. Nothing could be more offensive to me.*

A VISIT FROM GEORGE III

What with Sarah's prolonged absence from Blenheim after the death of her Duke, her daughter's indifference to the place and her grandson's neglect of it, the palace lost its lustre for royal visitors. But once the 4th Duke had provided the enthusiasm and the cash, Sir William Chambers and Capability Brown had wrought their magic inside and out, the palace was once more fit for

opposite The Temple of Health, made of limestone and Welsh slate, designed with classical Corinthian columns by William Chambers and John Yenn in 1789 to mark the recovery of George III from a mental illness. Inside is a medallion depicting the monarch and a polished marble tablet inscribed in Latin celebrating his recovery.

a king. Entertaining had, however, become something of a burden for the increasingly reclusive 4th Duke, and when it was announced in the summer of 1786 that King George III, who was after all a close friend, was to visit Blenheim, he panicked and had to be reassured by friends that all would be well. And of course it was. The royal party breakfasted in the Library, walked in the park, returned for cold meats and fruit, spent a whole hour looking over the principal rooms and "everything in them," the King remarking as he left, "we have nothing to equal this." He was right. Buckingham House, as it was then, was dull in comparison. The friendship endured. The two men shared a love of astronomy, the King gifting the Duke state-of-the-art telescopes. For his part, the Duke commissioned the Temple of Health to be built in Blenheim park to celebrate his friend's, albeit temporary, recovery from the madness that plagued him.

PARTYING WITH PRINCES

Edward VII was my grandfather's godfather, and he moved in the same circles as the 7th Duke, who entertained at Blenheim on a pretty lavish scale. The Prince of Wales, as he was styled then, stayed over several times for state dinners and dancing afterwards in the Long Library. Apparently, the Prince was a keen dancer and on one occasion, having danced all night, was still dancing the cotillion at four in the morning. He was a regular enough visitor for the First and Second Staterooms to be refurbished in white and gold in his honour. However, the Marlboroughs were not invited to the Prince's wedding in 1862 and relations cooled somewhat. There was a spectacular falling out when George Blandford, heir of the 7th Duke, eloped with the wife of the Prince's best friend. The Prince called out Blandford as the greatest blackguard alive, and things went from bad to worse, leading to the Marlborough family being effectively exiled to Ireland until the scandal died down.

The 9th Duke, Charles and his American wife, Consuelo, entertained very lavishly. The Prince of Wales, his wife, and his distinguished entourage featured often in the visitors' book; and, of course, Blenheim, at the time at its peak of magnificence, was the most suitable of venues for entertaining royalty … apart from the woeful lack of bathrooms.

GAME BOOK.

Season 1896-97

ER.	NAME OF BEAT.	NO. OF GUNS.	NAME OF GUNS.	Pheasants.	Partridges.	Hares.	Rabbits.	Duck.	Snipe.	Woodcock.	Moorhen.	Various.	TOTAL HEAD SHOT.
			Brought forward	73	626	103	2170						2972
	High Park	8	H.R.H. The Prince of Wales										
			Marquis of Londonderry										
			Earl of Gosford										
			Major Genl Ellis	82		1	1905						1988
			Hon George Curzon										
			Rt Hon Henry Chaplin										
			Sir S. Scott. Mr W H Grenfell										
	North Leigh Coverts	7	H.R.H. The Prince of Wales										
			Earl of Chesterfield										
			Earl of Gosford, Viscount Curzon	881			4						885
			Rt Hon George Curzon										
			Major Genl Ellis, Mr W H Grenfell										
	Monument Park	8	H.R.H. The Prince of Wales										
			Marquis of Londonderry										
			Earl of Gosford Sir S Scott										
			Earl of Chesterfield			1	3328						3329
			Major Genl Ellis Rt Hon H Chaplin										
			Mr W H Grenfell										
			Carried forward	1036	626	105	7407						9174

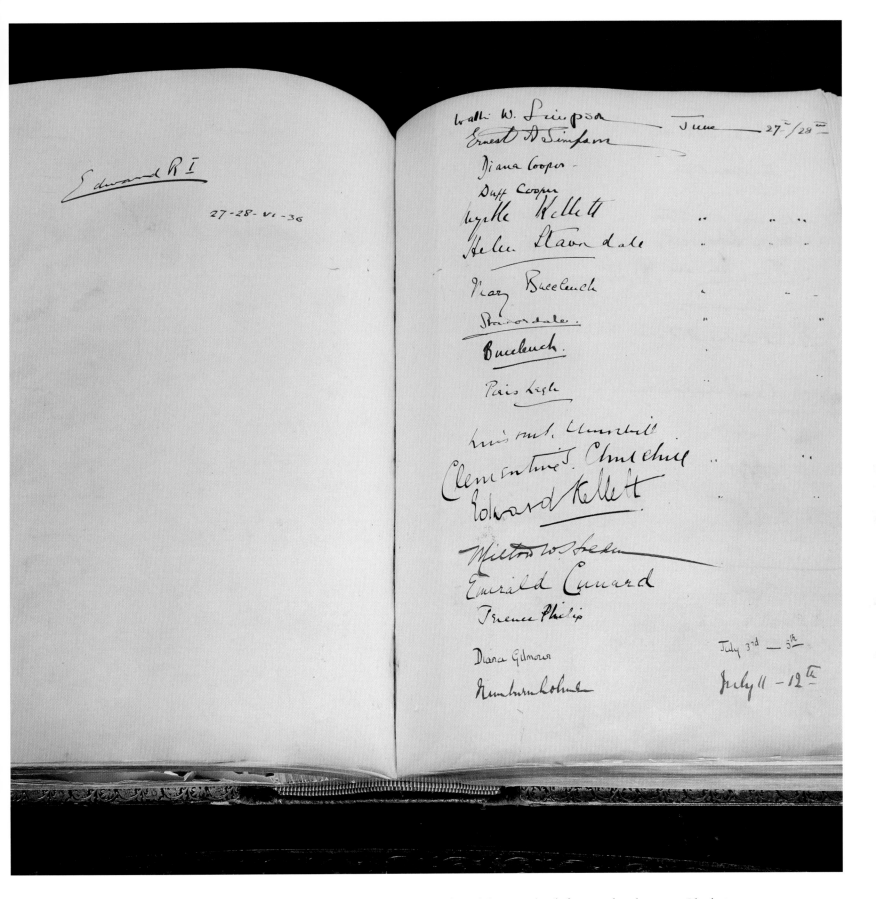

opposite Entries from the game book for the 1896–7 season lists Edward, Prince of Wales, the playboy son of Queen Victoria known affectionately as Bertie, as a gun. This famous shooting weekend, replete with illustrious guests, was talked about for decades thereafter.

above The guest book for a weekend party at Blenheim in June 1936. Edward R was the uncrowned Edward VIII. He was to abdicate six months later for the love of Wallis Simpson, who is listed among the guests on the facing page alongside her husband, Ernest, putting on a brave show for the gossips.

In my grandfather's and my father's time, connections between our family and the Royal Family were marked at family gatherings such as weddings and christenings and invitations to shooting parties at Blenheim and at Balmoral. Our private photo albums contain some charming, candid moments at picnics, barbeques, and other events. There are snapshots, too, of Edward VIII and Mrs. Simpson, relishing moments of relaxation among friends before the upheaval of the abdication. The Queen Mother, Queen Elizabeth II herself, Charles, the then Prince of Wales, and Princess Margaret (quite a favourite with the staff at Blenheim) were always welcome visitors.

H.R.H. Duchess of Gloucester
H.R.H. Duchess of Kent

above The little girl looking out in this photograph is our late Queen Elizabeth II, and the statuesque tall man with a cigar is my grandfather, Bert.

right A page from a family photograph album recording a holiday weekend in Balmoral at the invitation of the soon-to-abdicate King Edward VIII with Mrs. Simpson now confidently at his side. Tensions must have run high. Distractions included shooting, hiking, and picnicking in the hills.

His Majesty. Mrs Simpson.
Mollie.

BALMORAL.

Queen Elizabeth's Coronation, June 2nd, 1953

My aunt Lady Rosemary Muir (née Spencer-Churchill) had the honour of being selected to be one of the six maids of honour at her late Majesty's coronation. The invitation came from The Earl Marshall, The Duke of Norfolk, the criteria being that the young women had to be unmarried, tall, a daughter of a Duke, Marquis or Earl, and between the ages of nineteen and twenty-three. Aunt Rosie was very fortunate to fit the brief.

My aunt was twenty-three and engaged to her future husband, Robin Muir. They duly postponed the date of their wedding so she could fulfil the role. She recalls the Queen "being so confident", which in turn allowed them to relax, knowing they were in safe hands. She also recalls the Duke of Edinburgh "boosting morale" and just being a wonderful support.

Their lavish dresses of cream silk, embroidered with silver and gold thread, were made by Norman Hartnell, who also made the Queen's robe. With her wedding just a couple of weeks after the coronation, Aunt Rosie was rushing between fittings for her coronation gown and her wedding dress, which was being made by rival couturier Hardy Amies.

For many years, much to the consternation of my aunt, her coronation gown went missing. Teams searched high and low at Blenheim, knowing where it *should* have been stored but to no avail. Realising that there was to be much publicity for the Queen's Platinum Jubilee, another concerted search effort was made which, to huge sighs of relief all round, finally located the dress and off it was sent to be restored. In June 2022, the famously elusive dress, having been expertly repaired, was unveiled by presenter Nick Knowles to Aunt Rosie for an episode of the programme *Heritage Rescue*. Needless to say, Aunt Rosie was very moved, and she was prompted to give a series of interviews reminiscing on the magical day.

above right Aunt Rosie's Coronation maid of honour dress that was lost and subsequently found and restored.

right My grandfather and grandmother in their robes preparing for the coronation of George v in 1911.

opposite Aunt Rosie is the tall third maid on the left-hand side of the Queen.

Family Events

Both inside the house and outside in the park, events feature strongly as part of life at Blenheim. With such substantial grounds and magnificent rooms built for entertaining it would be a great shame for them to lie dormant and unused.

From a family perspective, many important and memorable milestones have been celebrated at Blenheim, and balls have featured prominently. There was a famous weekend party in November 1874 during which Sir Winston Churchill was born prematurely as his parents attended a shoot and a ball. The last blast of prewar glamour was the coming-out party of my eldest aunt, Lady Sarah, in 1939. And the coming-of age party of Uncle Charles and my first cousin, Serena Balfour (née Russell) in July 1962 made headlines as the huge success of the season.

My own coming-out ball, however, as far as I was concerned, was an event with no fond memories for me. It was given by my father to celebrate his fiftieth, my brother James's twenty-first and my eighteenth. By everyone else's account it was a superb evening, but I had just returned from living six months in Florence and nine months in Paris, studying languages, art and history of art, so I had not spent much time with my old schoolfriends and peer group, nor indeed in London, so I felt well out of the fold. My white dress had been selected by my then-stepmother, Rosita, and I didn't particularly take to it. The shoes, however (also white), I bought whilst I was in Paris with my dear friend Sophie Hapsburg, and, yes, they were super-stylish and sophisticated – the high point of my outfit. To be honest, I don't remember much detail of the evening: who I may or may not have danced with, or even where we had dinner. I think I retired quite early while others danced the night away.

Grand family weddings have very much been part of life at Blenheim, too, and although most of the dukes were obliged to get married in London as a matter of etiquette, and to make it easier for those notable guests expected to attend, it was the daughters – whose parents were expected to host and pay for the wedding – who would have married at Blenheim – myself included. In earlier times, the wedding day would have consisted of a traditional wedding service in the Woodstock church for family and close friends in the early afternoon. A large reception at Blenheim would follow, where many

The last blast of prewar glamour was the coming-out party of my eldest aunt, Lady Sarah.

opposite above My aunt Sarah dressed to party. She was seventeen years old, and the world was on the brink of war.

opposite below My wedding day. I was married in the Woodstock Church, supported by my father. My dress was by the late designer, Sir Hardy Amies.

above My cousin Serena taking a moment before the festivities of her 1962 coming out ball in front of the portrait of our great-grandmother, Consuelo Vanderbilt.

dignitaries, extended family members and friends, tenants, estate workers and so forth would be invited and typically served champagne and a traditional tea. This was the pattern my own wedding took, with our spectacular reception held in the Long Library following a very substantial receiving line. To be honest, mine and my husband's guests accounted for about twenty percent of the gathering, with the rest being my parents' friends or those obliged to be asked.

Times and traditions have since changed, with this generation expecting a lavish dinner and dance complete with band and discotheque following a church service. My own son, Max, was fortunate to also be married at Blenheim, generously supported and encouraged by James and Edla. We had a family lunch in the dining room, then a late-afternoon wedding followed by a wonderful reception in the Great Hall with champagne, canapes, and cake-cutting. Dinner in the Orangery was reserved for the couple's friends, with a table each assigned to myself and his father, while the dancing in a separate discotheque went on until the early hours.

My half-brother Edward's wedding to Kimberly Hammerstroem was in the middle of the very hot summer of 2018, and they chose to have a small chapel service followed by a wonderful reception in the Water Terrace gardens. Dinner then followed in the house. The huge number of guests dined at tables set up not only in the Long Library but into adjacent corridors. They had a spectacular custom-built structure off the Saloon for after-dinner drinks and dancing followed by breakfast at the break of dawn.

My nephew George and his bride, Camilla, chose to have their wedding in the gardens with a reception under the cedar trees. Dinner and dancing were held in a custom marquee overlooking the water terraces and lake, the perfect spot for a tumultuous firework display.

My late Uncle Charles, who sadly died in 2016, two years after my father's death, married his second wife, Sarah (née Goodbody), in 2014 in the Chapel at Blenheim. Lunch followed in the Orangery. What a memorable and happy family event that was, not least because Sarah had not been married before and because my father, who died just a month later, had lived to enjoy the day.

All our family weddings have been unique and memorable and the difference in the styles of the weddings just highlights how lucky we are to have such an extensive variety of spaces to accommodate not only our own family occasions but those of anyone who wishes to hire out the space to create their own special day in a very special place.

above left The 1990 wedding of my brother James to his first wife, Rebecca Few-Brown, who is mother to the current heir, my nephew George.

above right My son, Max, and my granddaughter Isla on the day of her christening in the Private Chapel.

Churchill Memorial Concerts

We have hosted many Churchill Memorial Concerts, established in memory of Sir Winston, as fundraisers for small local charities and for music therapy. I was chair of the event for a number of years, and the criteria for inviting a guest speaker to give the tribute was that they had known or worked with the great man. Of course, those still available to fulfil the brief were few and far between, so we took the view to extend the invitation to global statesmen who may have been influenced by his great legacy. Included in a memorable line up were President Valéry Giscard d'Estaing, President Mikhail Gorbachev, and my most popular coup, President Bill Clinton. These headline acts certainly made selling tickets an easy task, although dealing with their various entourages came with a load of challenges; in Clinton's case, not knowing until the last days if he would actually turn up (this was in 2003, just before the second invasion of Iraq).

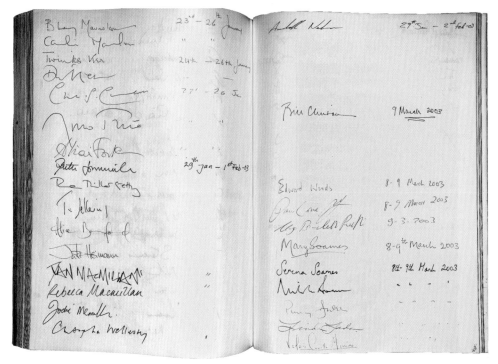

Distinguished speakers at the Churchill Memorial Concerts over the years.

above left Myself with a friendly Mikhail Gorbachev, last leader of the Soviet Union, Lady Soames, my father, and my stepmother, Lily.

above right Brian Mulroney, Prime Minister of Canada from 1984 to 1993.

left The guest book fills up with distinguished names on the occasion of the concerts, helping us raise a lot of money for local charities.

Good Works

Many of our more recent grand balls are focused on fundraising for charities. I particularly like to support local organisations, delighting in knowing that we can witness the benefits first-hand.

One of our most recent – and hugely successful – events was a ball in 2000 for the Oxford Appeal for Cancer Research, which raised over £200,000. In 2000 we threw a Blenheim Foundation Ball, which I helped my father to organise, inviting many of our wonderful American supporters to set up an endowment to fund vital restoration works at Blenheim. We are very fortunate to have the support of the US Blenheim Foundation, which has recently sponsored the renovation of our Chapel.

In 2018, my intrepid nephew, George Blandford, with three friends, competed in the Talisker Challenger, rowing across the Atlantic from the Canary Islands to Antigua. They completed it in a very fast time of thirty-five days. Not only did he raise huge sums of money through sponsorship for the Starlight charity (which supports the recovery of sick children through the power of play) but has continued to do so with biennial balls at Blenheim that have raised almost 2 million pounds. This is scheduled to be a biannual event, continuing to support such a worthwhile cause.

Earlier generations have also contributed to charitable causes in one form or another. Caroline (née Russell), 4th Duchess of Marlborough, in 1797 commissioned the building of almshouses in Woodstock to house widows and included a small endowment to keep the place up and running. This remained under the control of subsequent family members until 1968, when it was transferred to the Borough Council and renamed Caroline Court in her memory. Today it still provides sheltered accommodation for the elderly.

Fanny, the 7th Duchess, whose husband John Winston was Viceroy of Ireland, devoted her energies during their four-year stint in Dublin to helping raise funds for famine relief during the disastrous failure of the potato crops. Her work was duly recognised by Queen Victoria.

My great-grandmother Consuelo found suitable diversions from her unhappy marriage to Sunny in charitable causes. Feeling a strong sense of duty in her position of Duchess and *chatelaine* of Blenheim she took it upon herself to look after the poor local villagers and their children, even offering them work on the estate, much to the chagrin of Sunny, as he was not consulted. Having separated from her disapproving husband, she found a cause that touched her heart – the Church Army, similar to the Salvation Army, whose purpose was to train men and women to look after "destitutes" and give them a fresh start in life. Consuelo was charged by Prebendary Wilson Carlile, founder of the Church Army, to help him in a new venture to support and reinstate first offenders into public life so as to discourage them from a career in crime. She set about ensuring that the wives of prisoners were given shelter and employment, and throughout her life continued to focus on the welfare of women and children.

My grandmother Mary (née Cadogan) a no-nonsense, conventional and efficient lady was certainly the stuff that duchesses are made of. Her organisational skills were exemplary, whether arranging a ball for a thousand guests, entertaining royalty or preparing Blenheim for the unknown shadows of the Second World War, she went about all of it with ease. She became Chief Commandant of the ATS and the president of the Oxfordshire Red Cross, and along with my grandfather Bert ensured that both family and servants did their part for the war effort. It was during her time that the two famous Dior fashion shows were held at Blenheim. The first, in 1954, attended by Princess Margaret, was staged as a fundraiser for the Red Cross. It hosted 1,600 guests, who each paid five guineas to admire the latest Winter Collection. Four years later, in 1958, Blenheim hosted a repeat performance, with the same number of guests in attendance, only this time it was to admire creations by Yves Saint Laurent, who presided over the collections following Christian Dior's demise. Both shows raised around £8,000.

My father, too, was always very involved with local charities, acting as patron of many, and I have taken over the reins of some of these. One of his favourites was the Oxfordshire Boys Club (now Oxfordshire Youth), and from a young age I remember attending some fun fundraising events with him. One was a celebrity cricket match that was held for many years on the South Lawn at Blenheim and featured a team of celebrities against locals. Others involved local race nights, sponsoring fictitious horse or greyhound races while enjoying a lively supper with local friends. What strikes me now, looking back, is not only how important it is to instill in young people the importance of giving something back, but also how much more fun and sociable life was before the isolating effects of social media and TV.

Duchess of Marlborough Memorial Fund

Miss J. Airey	Mrs. Buckle
The Hon. T. J. Ashton	Mrs. Bull
Madame Balsan	Lord Cadogan
Miss Effie Barker	Mrs. Callis
Mrs. Barry	Lord Carnarvon
Miss M. Bartlett	Mrs. Carter
Lady Benyon, C.B.E.	Miss Cave
Miss Berry	Mrs. Cecil
Dr. F. Bevan	Mrs. Chalcraft
Mrs. Bland	Miss Chapman
The Marquis of Blandford	Miss J. Cherrington
Mrs. Bloomfield	Sir Winston &
Miss Bliss	Lady Churchill
Mrs. Booth	Miss M. E. Clarke
Mrs. Rupert Brett	Miss Clifford
Miss Violet Bridge	Miss E. V. Climenson
Miss V. Brooks	Mrs. Cooke
Miss Orde-Brown	Mrs. Crowe
Dame Ann Bryans, D.B.E.	Miss Cummins

opposite Walking Blenheim for Dior in 1954. The models made circuits of the staterooms and it was calculated they had clocked up three miles in the course of the day.

above Many were touched by Duchess Mary's generous spirit; after her death, this fund was raised for her favourite charities.

Keeping a Record

Many of my ancestors were avid recorders of their thoughts and deeds. The first to do this was Sarah, 1st Duchess, whose Green Book was full of her private thoughts about the wrongs that had been done to her. Most of her grievances were against her children. She opens the book with this statement:

> I desire this book may be given to my ancestors at my death. And I earnestly desire of them that they will preserve it and make use of it upon any occasion which may happen, to vindicate me.

Well, preserve it they did, and Sarah's book is safely in our archives.

The diaries of the 4th Duke are also preserved in the archives, and while not quite so well expressed, they are a meticulous day-to-day record of the health of the family – who visited, who dined, and how much money the Duke (as he refers to himself) won and lost. In a week spent in London in February 1774 he won 100 guineas and lost 390 playing Quinze, a card game similar to blackjack, at home and visiting Almack's, a high-stakes gambling club in Pall Mall.

While the 4th Duke's dairies are a bit abrupt, his recording of his scientific passions – astronomy and weather patterns – was meticulous, and his record books are a delight to behold with their beautiful, precise calligraphy. They are some of the most treasured items in our archives. He established the Blenheim Palace Observatory in the south-east tower of the palace around 1780 and learned how to use the latest astronomical instruments from Thomas Hornby,

above Sarah, the 1st Duchess, kept a little green book in which she recorded all her grievances, and she had many, mostly against the establishment, her surviving daughters, their husbands and her grandchildren. She had fire in her to the end.

right The gloomy scrawl of the prudish, religion-obsessive 7th Duke. Not a very uplifting read, the entries are a running commentary on his spiritual ups and downs.

opposite A ledger of planetary observations and recordings of weather patterns. Beautifully and clearly inscribed in several volumes by the scientifically-minded 4th Duke, who could have enjoyed a stellar career in the sciences if only he hadn't been a duke.

The 4th Duke's … meticulous record books are a delight to behold with their beautiful, precise calligraphy: an absolute treasure in our archives.

Example 5.ᵗʰ

Examp: in yᵉ Comparison of Count Bruhl's Timekeeper at Blenheim Jan:ʸ 6. 1782.

	H. ′ ″	♋	
Epoch for 1782	18 . 41 . 3 , 30	941	
Jan:ʸ 6 . .	0 . 23 . 39 , 30	1	Comparison of yᵉ Clock & Timekeeper
	19 . 4 . 42 , 60	942	Sidereal T. by yᵉ Cl. 22 . 9 . 25 , 0
Correction for the Equinoxes . . .	− 0 , 39		But yᵉ Cl. was too fast . . . . . 45 , 0
☉ M. Longitude corrected . .	19 . 4 . 42 , 21		True Sid: Time . . 22 . 8 . 40 , 0
True Sidereal Time . . .	22 . 8 . 40 . 0		The Timekeeper was 2 . 37 . 0 , 0
	3 . 3 . 57 , 79		
Correction for the ☉ motion . .	− 30 . 13		
Mean T. for yᵉ Merid:ⁿ of Blenth: 3 . 3 . 27 , 66			
For diff of Merid: betw D.Heb: & Blenth: + 4 . 52 , 0			
The Timekeeper should have shewn 3 . 8 . 19 , 66			
Time it did shew . . . . 2 . 37 . 0 , 0			
Timekeeper too Slow . . . 31 . 19 , 66			

Some Explanation of the Preceding Examples.

When the True Rᵗ: Asᶜⁿ: of the Moon, or any Planet or Star is found by observing its Passage over the Meridian it is the same as the Rᵗ Ascension of the mid-Heaven at the Time of Observation. Compute then the Mean Place of the Sun, as in the foregoing Examples, for the Noon preceding the observation & apply the Equation of the Equinoctial Points; & you will have the Mean Longitude or the Mean Rᵗ: Asᶜⁿ: of the Sun reckoned from the True

About this time I receiv'd a letter from Mr Weston Father to the Rector of Witney to desire I would forgive Bennett as he has made him all the satisfaction he desir'd — I wrote him word, that as he desir'd it — I would this time: I receiv'd another letter from him saying him man he was oblig'd to me &c and that he & his Son should be ready to obey my command at any time & in any thing —

Pay'd Child 1100 £ by a Receipt on Backwell —

on & for my intentions of giving the University my Great Telescope — N.B. these were transmitted to me through Mr Hornsby —

March 8.
Miss Dereguli. Mr Walker dined with us — Lost 420 G. at Almacks —

March 9.
Lost 450 guin at Almacks at Quinze —
March 10.
Rec'd of Backwell £525 —
Won at Almacks 100 guin —
March 11
Won at Almacks 85 guin.

who ran the Radcliffe Observatory. He later built another observatory in the south-west tower. Neither has survived. He shared his passion with King George III, who gifted him a ten-foot, state-of-the-art telescope made by astronomer Sir William Hershel, then president of the Royal Astronomical Society. This is no longer in our collection, and no one seems to know what became of it. He kept up lively scientific correspondence with leading figures in the world of astronomy and contributed much to the body of scientific knowledge.

The 7th Duke kept a record of his religious scruples in a set of beautiful notebooks, each page sombrely edged in black. It is hard to compute that when writing these journals he was a young man in his early twenties, recently married with a good position as the MP for Woodstock, and had an assured future ahead of him.

Oh my god what can I say? What heart so cold and sinful as mine? So ungrateful, so unaffected by thy love and infinite compassion, thy tender mercies … That latent love of the worldly of which I was unconscious of at the time and only this morning through God's goodness see fully and clearly … thou art answering my prayers in showing me the real state of my heart …

And so on. Not so much a diary as an endless monologue.

Theatricals

Going to the theatre was all the rage at every level of society in the eighteenth century. Theatres proliferated in cities and towns and featured witty plays addressing the social conditions of the time, usually followed by a fall-about farce. It wasn't long before the aristocratic owners of great houses thought to create private theatres of their own. Duchess Caroline, wife of the 4th Duke, was keen to introduce her children to the joys of home-grown theatricals, and it hadn't escaped her attention that performances at Blenheim would attract quite the right kind of crowd to plays and supper parties. And she had five daughters of marriageable age to consider.

In 1787 the theatre was created within Vanbrugh's Conservatory on the south side of the Kitchen Court, now the Orangery. The stage was situated at the east end of the conservatory, above it the sign: "Laugh where you may, be candid where you can."

Cast members were mainly family, augmented with friends and the occasional semiprofessional. The theatricals were a great success, giving purpose and busyness to young lives in danger of being blighted by idleness.

A regular visitor to Blenheim at this time was Edward Nares, an Oxford friend of Lord Henry. He was a passably good actor and soon became a very popular guest, invited again and again during the theatrical season. Described as very short and sprightly with a large nose, he was an Oxford scholar, not at all well-born or wealthy, and destined to become a vicar. In 1789 he appeared in the play *The Deaf Lover* with Lady Charlotte. Something was kindled on that stage that kept burning brightly. The Duke and Duchess were adamantly opposed to any hint of a relationship between their daughter and a penniless vicar. After the tragic death in 1795 of Lord Henry, Charlotte's brother and Edward Nares's dear friend, Charlotte, the Duke's favourite daughter, defied her parents and left Blenheim forever, walking from Blenheim to Oxford into the arms of Edward Nares. They were married, had two daughters and lived in a small vicarage, but they weren't to live happily ever after. She was banned forever from Blenheim, chiefly by her mother, the proud Duchess. Charlotte died in 1802, aged 33. Once the proud Duchess had died, the Duke relented, welcoming the widowed Edward and his granddaughters to Blenheim and reinterring his daughter in the family plot. Their story is worthy of a screenplay.

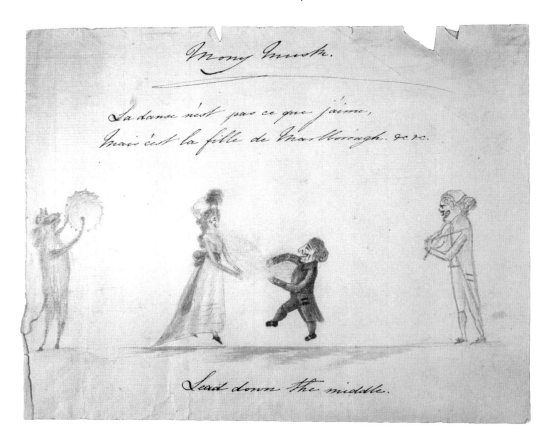

opposite The diaries of the 4th Duke are an entertaining glimpse into eighteenth-century aristocratic life. The diaries record a lot of dining, gambling, hunting and shooting, and health concerns.

left The passion of the short and beaky-nosed Reverend Nares for Lady Charlotte, observed in this sketch by her brother, Henry. There is a prescient line from one of the plays spoken by a Spencer daughter: "You can see what an excellent actress I should have made if fortune had not unluckily brought me into the world an Earl's daughter."

Cards, Gambling and After Dinner Games

After-dinner games were somewhat of a tradition in English country houses, often instigated by the ladies as the men lingered over their port and gossip in the dining room. After-dinner fun ranged from card and board games, backgammon, chess, cribbage and checkers to music-making, dancing and play-acting.

Whist, the forerunner to bridge, was perhaps the most popular card game in the eighteenth century and generally, as far as the women were concerned, did not involve gambling. Piquet, sometimes known as cent, has been popular on and off in Britain since the seventeenth century until the far simpler and less highbrow game of gin rummy came along. Sarah, 1st Duchess, was known for her skill at hazard, a gambling contest played with two dice that has been mentioned as far back as the fourteenth century. She rarely lost.

At Blenheim we have always had a card table set up; often two if there is a large weekend house party. Since as long as I can remember both bridge and gin rummy were played regularly between tea and changing for dinner and again after dinner. Small wagers were usually pledged with the high stakes placed not at home but in the gambling clubs. I always found the

bridge table quite intimidating, and although my mother taught me how to play as a teenager, I could never summon the courage to join a grown-up game, having witnessed the tempers if a contract was not made. Bezique was another favourite of our family, originally played with one or two packs until the six-pack version using cards from the seven to the ace was made popular by Winston Churchill. It is still a game I play at home with my sons.

Any large English country house would not be complete without a billiard room with a full-size twelve-foot table covered in green baize with six pockets (if playing snooker, twenty-two balls are used, as opposed to fifteen in billiards). I am not sure that many families were actually ever taught the skills of the game, and it is only by years of playing and practise that expertise is achieved. When played at Blenheim, a game may start out as a competitive snooker game but soon ends up as a more riotous game of Freda, where players run around the table trying to keep the red ball in play by hitting it with the white ball. Hugely fun with teenagers and beneficial exercise after a heavy dinner.

A Combination Game of Whist.

opposite A table temptingly set up for card games or poker in the corner of the Grand Cabinet.

left Henry, second son of the 4th Duke, was a dab hand at caricatures. Here he has drawn a lively scene of portly, bewigged gentlemen playing a round of whist. There is money, or at least tokens, on the table.

Betting was always popular among the men, originating from fairs and animal fighting held in local pubs with names such as Ye Old Fighting Cocks or the Dog and Duck, where bets were made over pints of beer on which cock or animal might survive a provoked fight. This adrenaline rush of raw excitement migrated to the gentleman's clubs and the sporting grounds where bets were laid on everything from rolling dice and card games to horseracing. Many clubs and coffeehouses morphed into private members' clubs where the aristocracy could meet like-minded people to socialise, conduct business, and gamble in a safe environment without the beer, blood and flying feathers. To be a member of a reputable club such as White's, Brook's or Almack's was essential to a man's standing to move forward in life, and often the choice of club came down to political leanings or the school, university, or regiment attended.

From the 4th Duke's diaries it was clear that he was an avid gambler, and, being meticulous by nature (some would say obsessive), he recorded every gain and every loss and where they took place. I am sure there were many other dukes and close family members who participated as much, but sadly we do not have the records to summarise and compare.

Most recently it has been horse racing that has tempted my family into the betting world, not only because of our passion for any sport involving horses but because it also has the social element – Royal Ascot, Cheltenham or the Derby – which adds immensely to the allure.

right An after-dinner game of cards for Clementine Churchill and a fellow guest at Blenheim.

following pages The Billiard Room has moved location several times. In 1886 the table was in the Red Drawing Room, surrounded by priceless tapestries and precious objects. Now it's located on the private East Wing next to the China Room.

… two grown men would appraise the formations (of the lead soldiers) and complain about the lack of artillery support.

Collecting

The most famous collection, the largest and most important of all eighteenth-century collections, the stuff of legend indeed, were the Marlborough gems. The 4th Duke put together this amazingly valuable collection of more than 800 pieces. The gems have images carved into gemstones, including garnets, sapphires and emeralds and cameos (carved into shell or into minerals such as agate and onyx). The Duke is ranked alongside Lorenzo de Medici, Empress Catherine II of Russia, and Peter Paul Rubens as one of the most important and influential collectors of engraved gems in history. Such a shame then that the whole collection was sold by the 7th Duke at auction in 1875 to raise money to repair the fabric of Blenheim. The entire collection was sold for £35,000 (over £5.5 million today) and then dispersed piecemeal by Christie's, so it is impossible to say where the gems have ended up. Luckily, records were kept of them, but all we have left are sketches and plaster casts. We are not in the market to buy them back as we are concentrating on re-acquiring instead, when funds allow, the dispersed artworks and paintings.

The 5h Duke's passion was for women, for extravagance, but also for books, especially ancient missals – and for exotic plants. And let's not forget about wine: his cellar at Whiteknights contained, rumour has it,

12,000 bottles. He spent a total of £60,000 on his gardens – that's over £8.5 million in today's money – with not much to show for it. His books and artworks were sold off by bailiffs along with Whiteknights, and its contents, including 100 pairs of shoes and 200 pairs of leather breeches. He was left, at the end of his life, all alone in a corner of Blenheim, where he died surrounded by bailiffs.

On a happier note, we have at Blenheim a magnificent assembly of 780 hand-painted lead soldiers made by the French master Lucotte, all in mint condition. These are not Winston Churchill's own collection – which are all British and now on display at the Cabinet War Rooms – and which he credits with "turning the current of my life … henceforward all my education was directed to passing into Sandhurst (Military Academy)." These are French regiments that belonged to a lifelong friend of Winston's, the French painter Paul Maze. Maze had them displayed in his London home, where the two grown men would appraise the formations and complain about the lack of artillery support. In 1935 Churchill and Maze spent Christmas together at Blenheim, and Maze, appreciating the potential for display at the palace, gave the entire army to my father, who was then just nine years old.

opposite These massed regiments of lead soldiers made by the French company Lucotte (which is still going strong) and collected by Paul Maze, an artist friend of Winston Churchill, were given to my father when he was a boy.

above The Marlborough gems were lovingly collected by the 4th Duke and sold off by the 7th Duke to fix the roof. All that is left of the amazing collection of exquisite carved gemstones is their memory,

preserved in sketches done as drawing practice by the children of the 4th Duke. Occasionally, one will pop up at an auction house, like a sapphire ring with an image of Julius Caesar that sold recently for £62,000.

An Artistic Streak

Artistic talents manifest themselves in different ways, through drawing, painting or sculpture, playing a musical instrument, creating a beautiful garden or house or indeed writing. It is difficult to know how much is in the genes or how much is learnt and absorbed through personal choice and interests.

We are not a musical family, certainly not on the Spencer-Churchill side; although my mother's side, the Hornbys, were more so. Looking through the talents of some of my ancestors there is certainly a strong sense of appreciation of art and architecture backed up by a power and desire to produce it in one form or another.

My ancestor Sarah Churchill clearly had a great sense of aesthetic that, coupled with being a savvy businesswoman, allowed her to make prudent and inspired decisions. Sarah's decision to not allow Sir James Thornhill to paint the Saloon walls and ceiling but selecting Laguerre instead led, in my view, to a more interesting and varied result. From sacking Vanbrugh and employing Hawksmoor in his place led to a more completed interior with elaborate plasterwork and fitting tributes to John.

From records and retained paintings we know that Diana Spencer, the sister of the 4th Duke, was an accomplished artist who painted not only self-portraits but those of her children, as well as theatrical scenes. Her brother George, the 4th Duke, was a man of taste, and we were fortunate that he had plenty of funds to spend and that he spent them wisely. For the house he commissioned the skills of Sir William Chambers and in the park his collaboration with Capability Brown produced a spectacular landscape.

It seems that most of the 4th Duke and Duchess's children had a talent for drawing and whether this was as a result of endless tutoring in the subject or just talent, who can tell, but the results are there to see in their interpretations of the Marlborough gems, both as silhouettes or illustrated cameos. Both Henry, his second son, and his favourite daughter, Charlotte, were talented artists in different ways. Henry preferred to depict scenes as cartoons or people as caricatures, while Charlotte, clearly more of a realist, painted picturesque scenes of landscapes and sketches of people, showing a great maturity of skill beyond her years.

opposite Works by the talented Charlotte Spencer, the 4th Duke's favourite child, who eloped with an impoverished vicar and died young: A silhouette (*top*) of her father, the 4th Duke (who, incidentally, was red-green colour-blind); a landscape; and a pencil drawing.

above A charming painting of two of her daughters by Diana Spencer, sister of George, the 4th Duke. Diana was a talented artist with an interesting reputation, which only served to further her career as a painter and designer. Divorced and widowed, she helped to support herself with her art.

Although not a descendant of the family, Susan Blandford, wife of George (later 5th Duchess and daughter of the 7th Earl of Galloway), perhaps because of her husband's passion for gardening, developed a love of painting floral watercolours, which she executed with great talent. No doubt she had been privy to the rare species he had imported and was cultivating at their home, Whiteknights. Subsequently at Blenheim she spent her free time wisely, and we are lucky enough to own the originals which are still in a leather-bound book.

It is not clear whether the 6th Duke or his offspring were blessed with artistic talents as all records were destroyed; but moving on to the 7th Duke, it seems that his focus was on politics and religion rather than on the arts. Their grandson, Winston, was fortunate to be blessed with many talents: first and foremost public speaking, as he was someone whose skills and sense of conviction could portray his views and ideals to motivate and inspire people to great effect. He was also a prolific writer, not only recounting current history but he also had a wider view, and a scholarly sense of perspective. As if that wasn't enough, Winston was an accomplished painter. I think his gift as a painter started out as a hobby, a way of escaping from the tough world of politics and as an antidote to his bouts of depression. He was first introduced to it by his sister-in-law, Gwendoline, who was an amateur artist, and from there his skills developed with the encouragement of his friends Paul Maze and Sir John Lavery. He went on to paint many noteworthy scenes from home and his travels abroad.

My great-grandfather "Sunny" the 9th Duke had a great sense of style and aesthetic too. Whilst it is a well-known fact that he married Consuelo Vanderbilt for her large dowry, it is fortunate that both spent it wisely, ensuring that the house was modernised for the twentieth century and the formal gardens enhanced to provide backdrops suitable for a palace.

Consuelo and her mother, Alva, were both well-educated and had a love of Paris in particular. Thus, many of the furnishings we still enjoy today are a result of her good taste and the suppliers and craftsmen that she relied on from Paris and beyond.

Both my grandfather and father didn't necessarily have direct artistic attributes, although they both had

S. Blandford.   Phlox subulata

a sense of how to entertain in style and treated their guests to lavish weekends of entertainment and luxury. They both had a love of the outdoors and probably paid more attention to enhancing the gardens and landscape with tree-planting and reinvigorating neglected areas of the park.

From my generation, my brother James used to be artistic at school, and I remember well pieces of woodwork he brought home that were not only well made but practical. I have never been a gifted two-dimensional artist, but I have always loved art and found the three-dimensional art of sculpture more appealing. Over the years, when I have had time, I have attended life-modelling classes and have dabbled in wood-carving, which resulted in many cuts and hands covered in bandages, but I found both processes very therapeutic and satisfying. Of course, my main love has been houses, the architecture and the art of designing the interior to make a home. Perhaps when I have more time I will revert to sculpture and maybe pottery, and even gardening, but, unfortunately, I don't think music or learning an instrument will hit my bucket list or come to the surface as a hidden talent. I just don't have the genes.

opposite A botanical drawing by Susan Blandford, subsequently the 5th Duchess, who shared an interest in botany and rare plants with her philandering husband.

this page A landscape by Winston Churchill, a man of multiple talents, hangs above a bust of the great man, sculpted in 2017 by Hamish Mackie. The painting is a view of Marrakesh, painted in 1947.

SIR WINSTON CHURCHILL
HAMISH MACKIE 2017

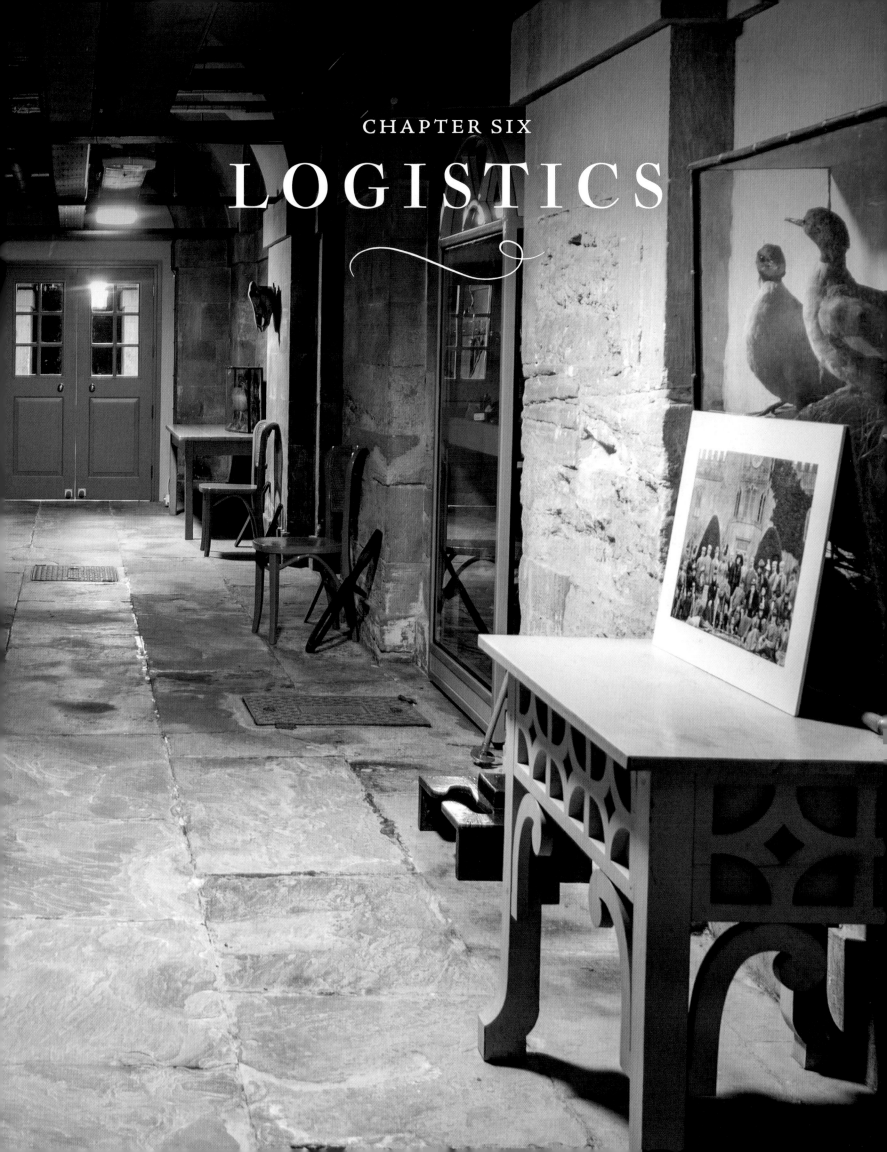

CHAPTER SIX

LOGISTICS

BLENHEIM PALACE BELLS

	NAMES ON BRASS PLATES	MODERN NAMES	
Nº 1	East Bedroom Nº 5	3ʳᵈ BACHELOR'S ROOM	Nº 1
Nº 2	East Bedroom Nº 6	4ᵗʰ BACHELOR'S ROOM	Nº 2
Nº 3	Dukes Garden Door	Duke's Garden Door	Nº 3
Nº 4	Dukes Sitting Room	Duke's Sitting Room	Nº 4
Nº 5	Entrance Gates	Entrance Gates	Nº 5
Nº 6	Tenier's Room	Duke's Bedroom	Nº 6
Nº 7	Tenier's Bedroom	State Bedroom	Nº 7
Nº 8	Bow Window Room	Private Dining Room	Nº 8
Nº 9	Duchess Room	Reynolds Room	Nº 9
Nº 10	Lady Louisa's Sitting Room	North Sitting Room	Nº 10
Nº 11	Lady Louisa's Bedroom	North Bedroom	Nº 11
Nº 12	Double Bedded Room	Small Nurseries	Nº 12
Nº 13	Yellow Damask Room	Sunderland Bedroom.	Nº 13
Nº 14	East Bedroom Nº 1	1ˢᵗ Font Bedroom	Nº 14
Nº 15	East Bedroom Nº 2	2ⁿᵈ Font Bedroom	Nº 15
Nº 16	East Bedroom Nº 3	1ˢᵗ Bachelor's Bedroom	Nº 16
Nº 17	East Bedroom Nº 4	2ⁿᵈ Bachelor's Bedroom	Nº 17
Nº 18	Billiard Room	Small Library	Nº 18
Nº 19	Small Dining Room	State Drawing Room	Nº 19
Nº 20	Grand Cabinet	Grand Cabinet	Nº 20
Nº 21	Great Hall	Great Hall	Nº 21
Nº 22	Drawing Room	Billiard Room	Nº 22
Nº 23	Dining Room	State Dining Room	Nº 23
Nº 24	Water Court	Dean Jones Rooms	Nº 24
Nº 25	Coral Rooms	Coral Rooms	Nº 25
Nº 26	Waiting Room	Waiting Room	Nº 26
Nº 27	South Bedroom Nº 1	Blue Dressing Room	

LOGISTICS

A palace the size of Blenheim needs a whole lot of people to run it. When it was built there was no electricity, no gas and no plumbing— just people-power and scrubbing brushes. Cooking was done over open fires situated well away from the main building to minimise fire risk. Hot food had to be rushed along cold corridors to dining rooms, hot water carried up winding service stairs to bedrooms, and slop pails carefully carried down. There were fires to be laid, candles to be lit, silver to be cleaned, floors to be swept and tables to be laid. In the bedchambers there were clothes to be cleaned, aired, and laid out for wearing, shoes to polish, cosmetics and hair treatments to be concocted, mending to master and discretion to be maintained. In the laundry the daily drudgery of washing, rinsing, drying, starching and ironing was never-ending. In the nursery there were children to be fed, dressed, cared for and educated. In the park there were kitchen gardens and livestock to tend, flowers to grow, forests to manage, logs to cut, carriages and fire engines to maintain and horses to be cared for.

In the kitchen, work never stopped: fruit and vegetables from the estate had to be cleaned and prepared, meat butchered, game plucked and hung, bread baked, butter churned, milk cooled. There were meals to cook and serve to the duke and duchess and their guests, meals for the children, meals for the upper servants, and eventually a further sitting for the lower servants, who did the bulk of the physical labour and didn't get to eat until they had served everyone else. Then of course there was the washing up and the putting away. And then it all started again the next day.

Below Stairs

The 4th Duke and his Duchess had eight children and theirs was the first family to use Blenheim as a home. They employed eighty indoor staff and eighty outdoor staff. Numbers of staff fluctuated over the years; when times were lean, fewer staff were employed. At the end of the 4th Duke's life there were thirty-seven indoor servants, reduced to twenty-five by his profligate son, then cut back eventually to just fifteen. By 1821 most of the servants hadn't been paid for two years, but they at least had a roof over their heads and food to eat. The 6th Duke made a bit of an effort, but it took the 7th Duke to restore order. The arrival of gas and electricity eased the burden and the need for large numbers of indoor staff but added two electricians, or "men of science", to the wages bill. At the turn of the twentieth century, apart from the footmen and porters, the kitchen was managed by one chef with a staff of four, the household by a housekeeper with a staff of six housemaids, five laundry-maids and a still-room-maid responsible for cooking breakfast and making cakes. By 1939, in my grandmother's time, there were thirty-two indoor staff. By the time the Second World War was over, the staff count had dwindled to just eleven. In 1950 the palace was opened to the public and staff roles changed accordingly.

Today, Blenheim is a big business, and the estate employs about 450 staff in permanent and seasonal roles, ensuring that all is kept in good order, that events run smoothly all year-round, and visitors to the palace enjoy a unique experience.

previous pages Learning the bells: name changes are inevitable as rooms undergo changes of use and personnel. Lady Louisa for instance was one of the eight children of the 6th Duke. Her mother was his first wife of three, or four if you count a youthful elopement. No wonder staff kept to "Your Grace" and "Milady."

right The iconic bell system, now replaced by a telephone network. This was a busy hub. Breakfast, lunches, dinners and teas, would be carried up these stairs, through the hefty swing door at the top and then rushed along several hundred feet of corridor to the destination dining area.

The arrival of electricity eased the burden, … but added two electricians, "men of science", to the wages bill.

left Typically known as "the green baize door", the red leather door swings between the downstairs working world and the grandeur upstairs. It is designed so that someone carrying a tray can negotiate the transition easily – and spot someone coming the other way.

opposite A faded plan of the mezzanine rooms where personal servants to the household had their living quarters. They were low-ceilinged rooms tucked between the first and second floors. Proximity to their masters' or mistresses' rooms meant they were on call at all times and could appear and disappear as if by magic using the network of hidden stairs. There are no mezzanine rooms on the south side, as the staterooms to the south have very high ceilings and the rooms above need all the height they can get. A few mezzanine rooms have been turned into accommodations, and one even has an ensuite bathroom.

Terms of Employment

As part of their employment deal, servants of every rank had to be clothed, fed and housed, and their wages in hand reflected this. When the family were absent from Blenheim, or from any one of their other residences that were kept staffed, servants received board wages, a lower wage to cover the cost of their food – although servants in the country still had access to produce from the farms. There were perks too. Cooks were able to sell fat from the kitchen for the manufacture of ordinary tallow candles, and the butler could keep the ends of the high-grade wax candles. Butlers also could sell empty wine bottles, and ladies' maids were given their mistresses' castoffs to wear, to sell or to unpick and remodel.

Sarah, the 1st Duchess, was a kind and thoughtful employer and many of her staff stayed with her for years. She paid her butler £15 a year, the housekeeper £10, her chambermaid also £10, the Duke's valet £15, and the porters £8. Her hairdresser earned twelve shillings (60p) for a haircut, and there is an entry in the ledgers for a man who helped the 1st Duke clean his teeth. She left generous bequests in her will, bequeathing her chambermaid, Grace Ridley, £16,000, which would have been a fortune back then.

In 1772, the 4th Duchess had a full-time French hairdresser on £42 a year, a cook on £73.10s, another cook employed solely to serve Lord Blandford, the young heir, at £12 a year, and a fisherman on £60. Lowly maids and kitchen porters were on £8.

By 1812 cooks were worth £84, the butler £50, head gardener £50, the housekeeper £35, but the housemaids were still on £8.

The 9th Duke employed a cricket coach, a dancing master, a couple of wine specialists who came down once a week to stock the cellars, and French chauffeur on £16 a month to drive his motorcars. The First World War brought about massive societal change and increases in taxation that stripped about thirty percent of the revenue derived from great estates like Blenheim. As the 9th Duke presciently wrote to *The Times* in 1920: "The old order is doomed."

Wages in my grandparents' time between the wars were creeping up in line with inflation. The French chef earned £260 a year, and the housemaids were finally well into double figures on £50.

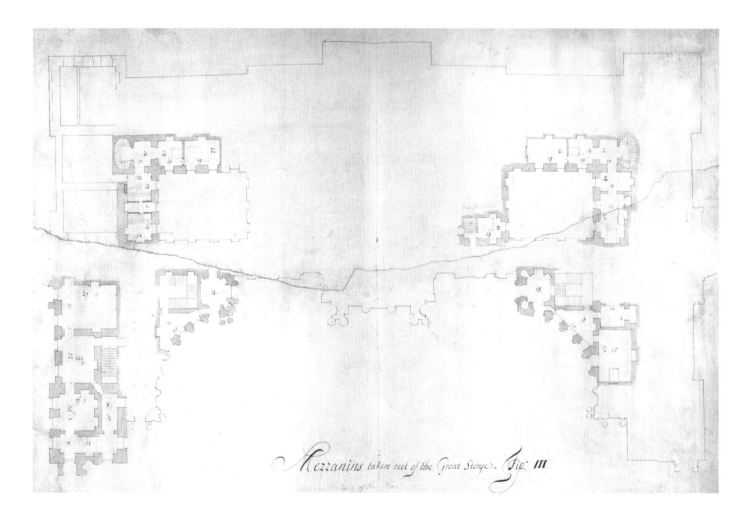

Mezzanins taken out of the Great Storye. Fig. III

ACCOMMODATION

Most of the army of servants were housed within the palace and some, including the gardeners, in various properties on the estate. Nursery staff had comfortable rooms near their little charges. Upper servants, such as the steward, butler, the cook and the housekeeper, had pleasant rooms on the second floor of the Kitchen Court. To be near their work, laundry and kitchen maids, bakers, and the gatekeepers also had rooms in the kitchen court. Coachmen, stable boys and grooms lived in the Stable Court. Housemaids and footmen slept up in the attic rooms of the palace, and the duke and duchess's personal servants had their accommodation in the low-ceilinged mezzanine above the principal floor, which had narrow spiral staircases leading to service doors within the principal suites so they could be summoned and appear in an instant. One element common to all staff accommodation was that the windows let in air and light but allowed no views of the grounds, nor of people coming and going. The windows were either set too high or too low to peek out of.

The little square windows between roof access and the grand arched windows are set high in the servants' bedrooms. Housemaids Heights are on the left, above the East Wing; the footmen over the West Wing in Postillion Heights.

Circular windows above the principal floor windows are set low in the rooms of the personal servants. The lower row is set high in the corridor that runs right round the undercroft of the palace, allowing servants access to every staircase, so they could magically appear where needed.

right and opposite Staff accommodation. The housemaids were tucked away in the attic. The male servants had a separate entrance to avoid chance meetings on the hidden stairs. The little round windows between the first and second floors bring light and air into the servants' mezzanine rooms, but are set too low for staff to peek out.

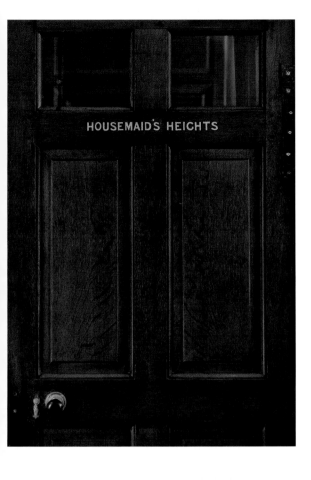

A floor plan of the kitchen block in the time of the 7th Duke. By this stage the kitchens had moved into the basement of the palace, making life a lot easier for the kitchen staff. What had been a greenhouse, and then a theatre, running along the south side of the court was now divided into offices, a gallery where the Duke hid paintings he considered too risqué for public view, and a Bakehouse which was to reduce his Titians to ashes. The dairy was situated in a cool corner on the north side, along with a special room for cheese. The laundry took up a lot of space, with a huge drying area. All domestic activity was hidden from the view of guests and family arriving and leaving via the impressive Flagstaff Gate by judicious positioning of colonnades and windows. The upper servants, such as the stewards, the housekeeper and the butler, had pleasant enough accommodation on the floor above.

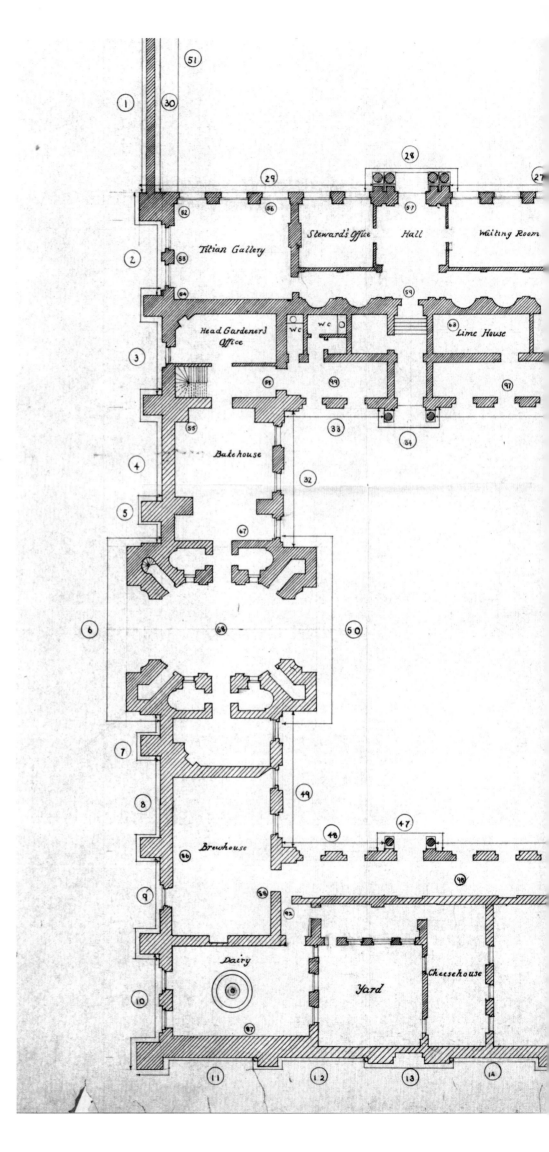

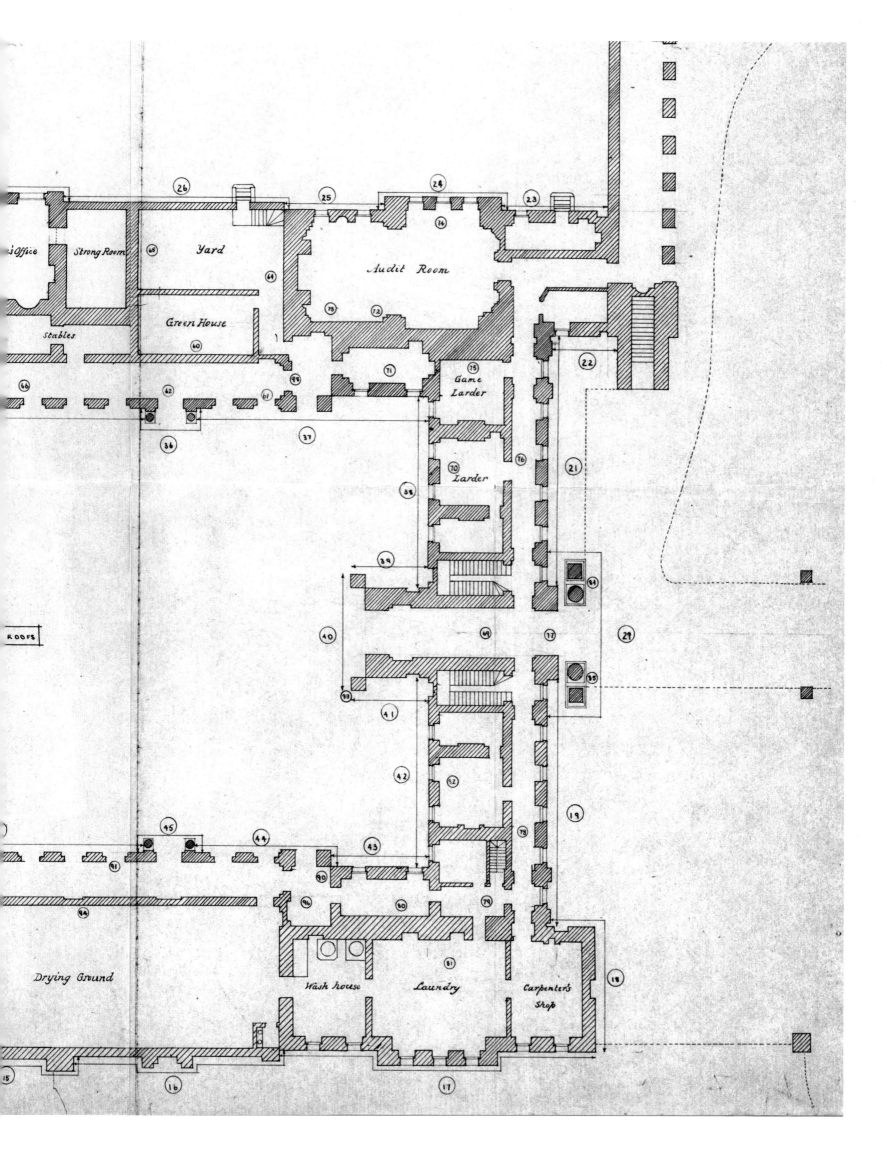

THE SERVANTS HALLS

At the time of building, Blenheim's servants could gather to take breath in the Common Hall, a large room at the northwest corner of the kitchen court, then furnished with two large tables and five benches. When the kitchens were moved to the basement of the main palace in the nineteenth century, the servants' dining hall moved there too. Maids and footmen had their own small sitting rooms and upper servants had their own private quarters in which to relax. Visiting staff accompanying important guests had to double up with Blenheim staff, which often did not go down well.

SUMMONED BY BELLS

In the early eighteenth century, the only way to summon a servant was to holler or to ring a handbell, so they had to hover in hallways and adjoining rooms. The invention of the bellpull in the early nineteenth century changed all that, giving the family their privacy back and allowing the servants to get on with their chores belowstairs while still being available to a summons. Wires ran from the handles in each room through wall and ceiling cavities to a bell board downstairs. The bells were mounted on pendulums that continued to swing, allowing the servants to see which bell had been rung. Each bell had a slightly different tone, and an experienced servant would know by the sound alone which room required service. The 8th Duke replaced the bells with an internal phone system of thirty-seven lines and a switchboard operator.

opposite, clockwise from top The realm of the butler. The basement wine cellar is vast, split into two—for red and white—and very well ordered. The mahogany cabinet on the table is a humidor to keep Winston Churchill's favourite Romeo Y Julieta brand of cigars in top condition. The butler's sanctuary, or pantry, where the silverware is kept in a safe and regularly cleaned. The original Butler's Sitting Room, a place to relax but also to work; there is a lot of paperwork involved in this job.

right Our present butler, Robin Willis, in the family sitting room, proffering a couple of very dry martinis.

Job Descriptions

STEWARD The most senior member of the household staff, the steward is basically management, responsible for the smooth running of the household, ordering and checking supplies, and keeping the household accounts.

THE BUTLER In charge of the male household staff, receiving guests, directing the service of meals, keeping and serving wine, overseeing the glassware and the plate.

GROOM OF THE CHAMBERS Charged with looking after the furniture and furnishings, quite a major job in a palace of nearly 200 rooms. He was also responsible for ordering newspapers and ensuring that every writing desk in every room is kept supplied with paper, pens, and ink.

THE HOUSEKEEPER Oversees all the female indoor staff. It is she who ensures that fires are lit, beds are made, laundry is laundered, and guests and family are

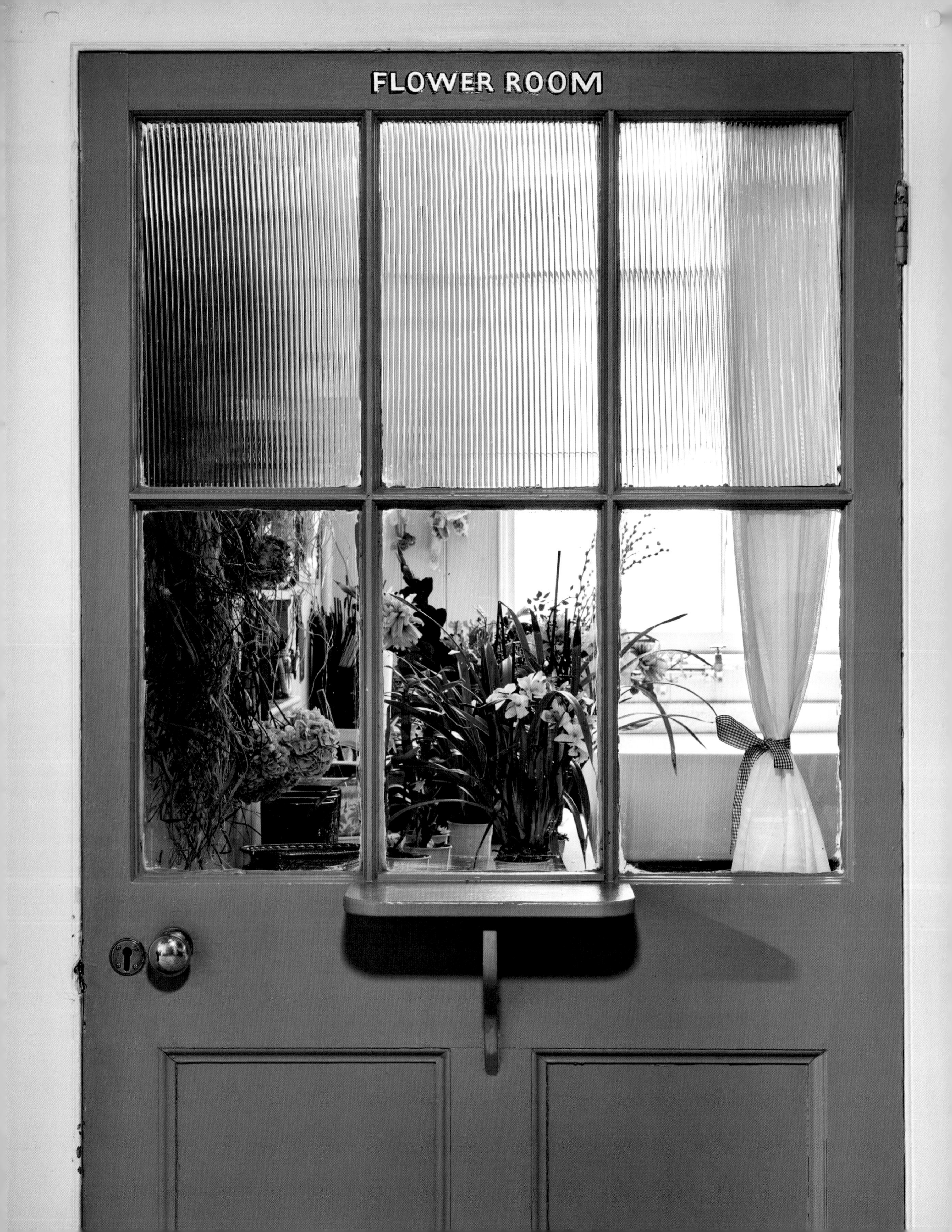
FLOWER ROOM

happy and supplied with hot water, clean towels, and chamber pots.

THE COOK Master or mistress of the kitchen staff, ordering supplies, cooking meals for the entire household and liaising with the butler over the way the food is presented and served in the dining room.

previous pages Copper pans in every possible size, along with moulds, biscuit cutters, and cake tins. Each one is embossed with the Marlborough crest and each one requires cleaning and polishing.

opposite In an ideal word every house would have a flower room and a pantry. When we have big events and weddings the planners bring in the most sumptuous floral assemblies, but down here in the flower room the cut flowers and foliage from our gardens are arranged to bring colour and life to the more private rooms of our palace.

above The nursery at Blenheim was much in use for my half-brother and sister. My brother and I were well past the nursery stage when our father inherited. The rooms are quite plain and simply furnished. "Functional" would be the word. There must have been fairly chaotic times in the past when the palace was alive with babies and toddlers and the nursery staff run off their feet with an unruly brood.

UNDERBUTLER A liveried servant (butlers wear sober suits) in charge of cleaning and polishing the silver, laying the table, and serving food and drink and late-night snacks.

NANNY, GOVERNESS AND NURSERY STAFF The Nursery and Schoolroom were a vital part of the aristocratic lifestyle, as the day-to-day care and early education of children was handed over to staff. In the eighteenth and nineteenth centuries, boys and girls were educated by governesses up to boarding-school age, then the boys were sent off to Eton and girls remained in the home schoolroom with the governess.

LADYS' MAID A woman who looked after the personal needs of her mistress. This would mean taking care of her clothes, shoes and jewellery, laying out appropriate outfits, dressing and undressing (more difficult than it sounds in the days of corsets, tiny, fiddly buttons, layers of underclothing and no zips). Add to that dressing her hair, running the bath, mending, giving manicures and keeping secrets.

VALET Performs the same personal role for his master, looking after all his clothes, shoes and choices of outfit. He also becomes privy to all his master's moods and foibles, which is where that old French proverb about no man being a hero to his valet comes from.

FOOTMEN Liveried staff whose job is to serve at table, answer service bells, move furniture, clean lamps, impress guests with their upright military presence and serve as valets when needed for younger men in the household.

HOUSEMAIDS, LAUNDRY-MAIDS AND KITCHEN PORTERS Staff who basically bore the brunt of the hard physical work involved in running a massive household, which was made so much easier as electricity, gas and proper plumbing became the norm. No more sooty fires, no more coal dust as the household entered the era of central heating and the vacuum cleaner. Washing machines and dishwashers made a huge difference to life belowstairs. But fine bone china, crystal, silver and gold plate can't go in the dishwasher and still have to be washed and carefully dried by hand. At Blenheim, precious things are hand-washed by the butler or underbutler in special large wooden sinks that will not damage the delicate tableware.

PORTERS There are two chairs with massive enveloping backs in the Great Hall, and these were for porters who were on duty 24/7. The backs are for shelter from the biting north winds. The main doors at Blenheim only open from the inside, so there had to be someone in the hall to open the door at all hours. But the main reason for the porters' presence was not a fear of intruders, but of fire. In a palace with myriad fireplaces and chimneys, candles everywhere and open cooking fires, the porters were an eighteenth-century version of a smoke alarm.

above right The perfect valet: shoes, socks, underpants, tie … every decision made and every outfit appropriate for the occasion, this one being for a shoot.

right A valet would ensure that the duke's clothes were laundered and ironed, dry-cleaned and aired, his shoes polished, mended, and resoled and his riding boots impeccable, waterproofed and well-buffed.

opposite At the end of the day, the valet and the lady's maid would be sure to turn down the bed, provide hot water bottles if necessary, and lay out clean nightwear. Time off was rare.

COACHMEN Liveried staff were outfitted with magnificent heavyweight coats and hats advertising their duke's presence on his travels. Their principal duties were to drive the coach and control the horses from an exposed position on a box seat. From the time of the 9th Duke, coachmen and postillions (mounted on one of the drawing horses) were replaced by chauffeurs and motor mechanics.

RUNNING FOOTMEN This was a position also made redundant with the advent of the motorcar. But the position has an interesting history, starting on the battlefield. Commanders and generals on horseback had no means to send messages to other positions on the field, so a footman would take the messages and run. Back home in peace time, the running footman would run beside the coach, helping to clear obstacles and, in case of emergency or breakdown (roads were very muddy and rutted), would run for help or to alert the next coaching inn along the route that it was time to prepare supper. They had a special livery that made running easier: lightweight shoes and a petticoat instead of heavy breeches. Rival dukes would gamble on the running prowess of their footmen. The 4th Duke devised a race from Blenheim to Windsor, he in a coach and four, the footman in his petticoat and running shoes. Needless to say the Duke won; the poor footman did his best and later died from exhaustion.

GROOMS AND STABLE BOYS They fed, exercised and cared for the horses and cleaned and maintained saddlery and harnesses. The grooms were expected to have a basic grasp of veterinary medicine and to teach the younger members of the family to ride.

opposite The private Boot Room entrance. From the outset, Blenheim was a working estate with a deer park. Hunting, fishing and shooting have always been part of life at Blenheim.

below Over in the stable block, in the days before the motorcar, grooms, stable boys and coachmen were kept very busy with a stable-yard full of hard-working horses and carriages that needed constant maintenance. Today, the horses, brilliantly looked after by an expert team, enjoy a life of sport and pleasure.

PARK AND GARDEN ATTENDANTS There are 2,000 acres of park and gardens to care for. Apart from the flower gardens and formal gardens, there are forests, a huge lake and hunting grounds. Working alongside an army of gardeners under the head gardener, including specialists in fruit and roses, were a fisherman, several gamekeepers, foresters, and huntsmen.

FIREMEN These were another vital part of the household staff. Fire buckets, water valves and hoses lined the servants' corridors in the basement, as kitchen and chimney fires were all too common. After a disastrous fire in 1861, Blenheim's staff were trained up into a fire brigade, receiving a supplement of £30 a year for this extra service. A brand-new Merryweather steam-powered fire engine was purchased in 1899 and the company even supplied the uniforms.

left A wonderful photograph taken by Gladys Deacon, the 9th Duke's glamorous, if temperamental, second wife. This is the army of gardeners assembled by the Duke and the landscape designer Achille Duchêne at the start of work on the water terraces.

above Part of the proud Blenheim Fire Brigade, with their steam-powered fire engine. Municipal fire brigades were first established in towns but properties out in the country had to rely on themselves.

following pages Precautions against fire were everywhere, especially near kitchens and chimneys.

Liveries

An impressive display of smart servants in matching outfits was a necessary sign of rank and distinction. At Blenheim, male servants were supplied with new costumes every year, and in 1st Duchess Sarah's time they were given a yearly allowance of twenty shillings to buy hats, shoes, and stockings. There were everyday liveries and then a further set of more elaborate outfits with silver braid, silver buttons, embroidered coats of arms and elaborate threadwork reserved for special occasions.

Inside the palace, the most visible servants were the footmen, whose jobs included serving at table, opening doors, and moving furniture around for the housemaids to clean behind. Given their secondary role as status symbols, it was obviously desirable to have matching footmen of good proportions who would fill out the tight-fitting uniforms to advantage. In those days tall footmen could command higher wages than their shorter colleagues. The 9th Duke insisted his footmen be six foot tall, and on formal occasions they had to powder their hair into sleek white caps (they were paid extra for the powder).

Outside servants included the coachmen, the postilions, and the porters who guarded the entrances, raised and lowered flags, and carried all manner of heavy things. These men, visible to all visitors, neighbours and inhabitants of the surrounding areas, were impressively and warmly clad in magnificent great coats and striking hats. Grooms and outdoor workers were also dressed in Blenheim colours, but in plainer and simplified versions, as were the chairmen, whose job it was to carry the 1st Duchess's sedan chair. Top servants, the stewards and the butler, were not liveried but wore extremely smart but sober versions of gentleman's clothing of the era.

Female servants often made their own clothes. In the mornings they would wear plain or print frocks with a white apron. As the day and the formalities progressed, they changed into smart dark dresses relieved with white caps, collars and cuffs, and maybe a pretty lacey apron.

Liveries were often made by the same Saville Row tailors who dressed their masters, with full attention given to detail and materials as the livery reflected directly on the standing of the household.

above right A footman's jacket for every day.

centre right and opposite The full ceremonial dress-to-impress footman's outfit, with silver tassels, silver buttons and intricate embroidery.

below right A warm, stylish coachman's coat.

DINNER

23rd January, 2020

Seared Tuna & Sashimi
Black Sesame
Asian Slaw & Wasabi

* * *

Roasted Veal Fillet
Goose Fat Potatoes
Heritage Carrots
Cavolo Nero
Red Wine Jus

* * *

Vanilla Crème Brulée
Fresh Raspberries
Sablé Biscuits

* * *

The Dining Experience

An enormous amount of staff time and effort goes into ensuring that meals are prepared, presented, served and cleared in a style befitting the magnificent surroundings of a palace, using the beautiful silver, china and glassware that has been accumulated through the generations. Butler, underbutler and footmen are all involved in this front-of-house service, from breakfast in bed to family lunches, picnics at Royal Ascot, grand dinner parties and teatime snacks. There is no kitchen on the private side, so it is not possible for a family member to rustle up a lunch or a quick supper.

HOW TO LAY A TABLE

Laying a table is all about the rule of the thumb. Start the setting with the central plate, ensuring the rim of the plate is an inch from the edge of the table (an inch is the first joint of the thumb). Cutlery is also lined up with the base of the knives and forks an inch from the edge of the table. The diner works his or her way from the outside to the inside, so starter cutlery is on the outside. Butter knives are placed on or near the side plate on the left, desert cutlery at the inner edge, closest to the plate. Wine glasses and water glasses are set on the right in a triangle. Menu cards and salt and pepper shakers should be within reach or sight of every diner.

SILVER SERVICE

While chefs in restaurants hover over each plate leaving the pass, ensuring that their work of art is delivered exactly as planned, in great houses the cook and the butler will confer as to how to present individual portions of food on one large platter. The butler or footman serves each guest individually from this large platter, starting with the guest of honour or the host. They serve from the left-hand side of the guest and clear from the right.

At the end of the main course, the table is cleared of salt, pepper and sauces. There is often a fruit course served before pudding. There's a lovely story about my father and his pride in the Blenheim peaches. He had this strong belief that these precious peaches should not be touched by human hands until selected by the person who was going to eat it (from a gold plate with a gold knife and fork). The peaches were harvested only when perfectly ripe by snipping the stalk and letting the peach settle into a cotton-wool-lined fruit box. The fruit box was then presented at table, with my father keeping an eagle eye on the guests to make sure that if their hands hovered near a peach, that was the peach they actually took.

pages 324 and 325 The China Room in the basement is a lovely, bright, purpose-built room for displaying and storing all the various china services, making it easy to choose the right plate style for the right occasion. We often set it up for an informal lunch.

previous pages and right A table setting for a formal dinner with the warm glow of silver and the gleam of glass. Menu card holders and salt and pepper all come with the Marlborough crest. The plates bear the Double M and the Ducal crown. This service has seen much use and may be in line for regilding round the edges.

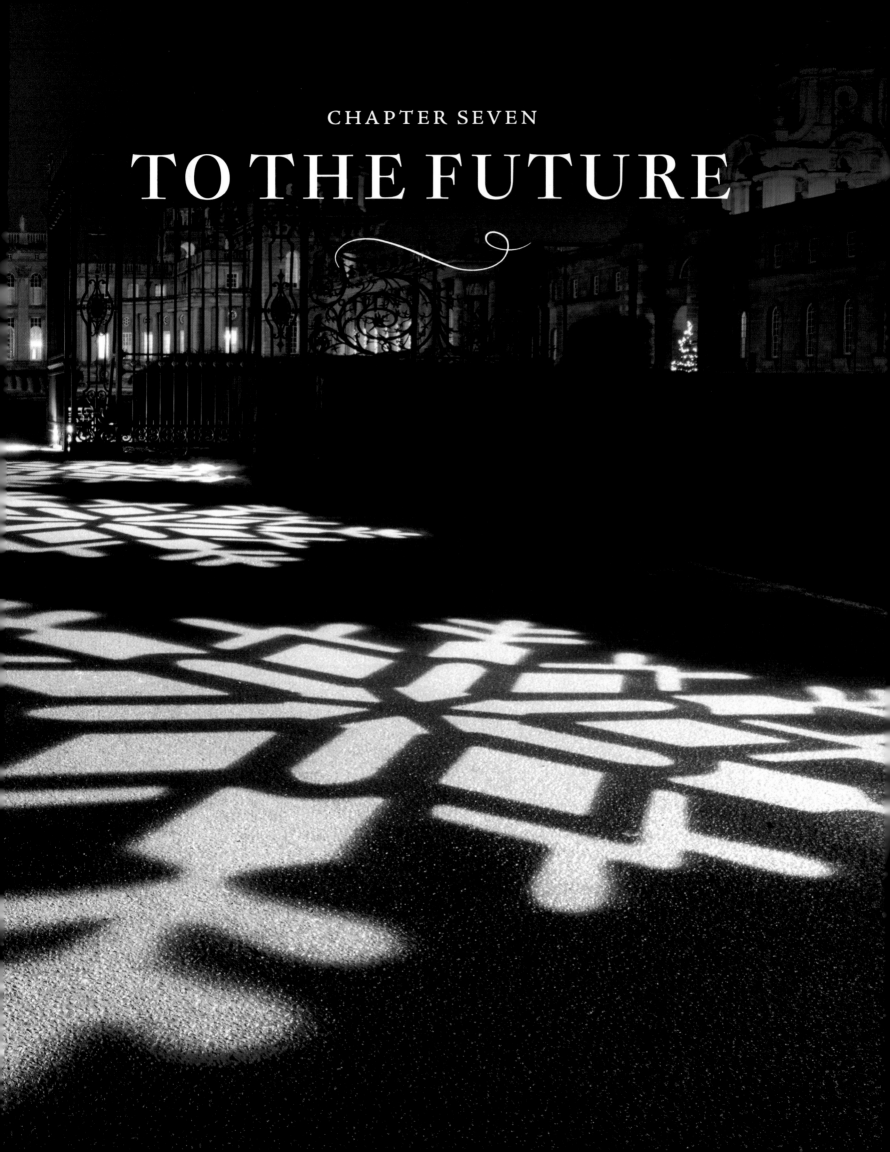

CHAPTER SEVEN

TO THE FUTURE

LOOKING TO THE FUTURE

The past decade has seen some major restoration work at Blenheim. It is always an interesting challenge to remake the work of master craftsmen (and they were men back then) in the spirit of the original but using modern techniques and state-of-the-art materials to ensure longevity. It means a lot of research and experimentation because there is often only one chance to get it right. All restoration work at Blenheim is carried out to the highest of standards, and it is our obligation to this historic Grade I monument and World Heritage site to recreate the designs and intentions of the original makers.

It is very important for us to share our magnificent heritage and make sure we have provided all necessary amenities – from restrooms to restaurants – for the huge number of visitors to the palace. We have talented teams at work throughout the palace, constantly caring for the fabric of the building, the landscape, the lake, the bridges, the statuary and the temples, as well as inventing and building wonderful new attractions and events to keep the experience of visiting Blenheim fresh and exciting.

previous pages Snowflakes projected on the Great Court: this is Blenheim dramatically dressed for Christmas as part of the Christmas Light Trail.

opposite Restored wallcoverings in the Indian Room. The panels had to be carefully removed and stripped of old glue, and the stains steamed out.

The Chapel

The Chapel was incomplete when John Churchill died in 1722, but Sarah was determined that it should be a fitting tribute to her hero husband, so she set about commissioning William Kent to design the magnificent marble tomb. This has always been the centrepiece of the Chapel and is perhaps more significant than any religious element.

Over many years, environmental fluctuations have caused significant damage to the building, resulting in damp walls and flaking paint and plaster. Coupled with the lack of lighting and heating, the space was not particularly inviting. Following my father's death (he is buried in the crypt below), I was determined

that the Chapel should be restored to its former glory. We set about doing research into stabilising the environment by adding doors, carrying out paint analysis to produce a colour scheme closest to the original, and choosing suitable lighting that would enhance the architectural details and monuments.

We were extremely fortunate and grateful to have the support of our American Blenheim Foundation, which generously funded much of the cost in memory of my father. The result is spectacular. We hope the chapel can now be used on a more regular basis, not only for family occasions but for fundraising events like concerts.

left and opposite The Chapel, restored to its former glory, generously sponsored by our American foundation. Repainting over 300-year-old plaster and historic layers of paint required much care and research. A milk-based casein paint was used to bond the layers to create an even consistency, while allowing the walls to breathe. The ceiling was painted a brighter white than the walls to reflect light. The Chapel has been reconfigured several times over the centuries. The altar was moved to its present position in the early eighteenth century and the pews, panelling, and pulpit are Victorian.

following pages The marble was cleaned and restored and the heraldic crests repainted.

The Orangery

Overlooking the Italian Gardens, the Orangery has had many uses over the years. It was built in the early eighteenth century to create a temperate climate for exotic plants and to grow oranges and lemons. During the 4th Duke's era it was turned into a 200-seat theatre where he and his eight children put on plays. During The 7th Duke's tenure it was used as an art gallery and was referred to as the Titian Gallery. Unfortunately, in 1861 a fire broke out in the Bakehouse next to the gallery and spread to the roof, which was ultimately destroyed along with valuable paintings. The glass roof was replaced in 1862 using the latest in glass-and-steel technology. The Orangery reverted to being a greenhouse until the 1980s, when its prime function became a restaurant and hospitality venue. In 2023, with the glass roof coming to the end of its life, coupled with the challenge of hotter summers and colder, wetter winters, we obtained the endorsement of Historic England to replace the roof with a timber and slate structure that will be more practical and last for many more years.

RUINS OF THE TITIAN GALLERY, BLENHEIM PALACE, VIEWED FROM THE GARDEN.

above The devasted ruins of the Titian gallery, which had been situated at the west end of the original greenhouse building.

right The Orangery as it is today – a glorious and practical light-filled venue overlooking the Italian gardens, used as a daily restaurant and also for functions.

Looking after the Lake

It had been more than 100 years since the lake had been dredged, and as a result the quality of the water and wildlife within it was suffering, so something had to be done. To restore the lake to around two metres of depth, more than 300,000 cubic tons of silt was removed and redistributed to an area north of the park that will eventually be returned to grassland. This involved using diggers set on a floating platform and installing temporary roads to carry the silt. The project took around two years to complete, but the result speaks for itself with its sparkling water and wildlife happily re-ensconced.

The Green Writing Room

A large crack was found in the ornate and heavy ceiling and cornice of the Green Writing Room, and it had to be urgently addressed. The crack was caused by movement in the fabric of the building. To gain access and safely carry out the essential repairs, which involved re-joining the cornice to the wall and existing timbers, the floor of the room above, the Sunderland Bedroom suite, had to be taken up. This was no mean feat as it required moving out all the furniture, including a large four-poster bed, wall tapestries, and other furniture. The bedroom floor is herringbone parquet, which had to be lifted and replaced in its entirety using the correct type of wood and to a design as close as possible to the original. The bedroom and Green Writing Room had the paintwork redone, but when funds allow there is more work to be undertaken.

For the duration of the works, a temporary tunnel was created as a walkway so the public could continue to view the remainder of the staterooms (because they all lead into one another). Above the protected tunnel, work continued on the ceiling, accessed by a huge scaffold.

Gladys's Eyes

Gladys Deacon was the second wife of the 9th Duke. She was French-American, a free spirit, and renowned for her beauty and intelligence. By the time she married "Sunny," her beauty had somewhat waned, but she was determined to leave her mark on Blenheim. She commissioned enlarged copies of her startling blue-green eyes to be painted on the ceiling of the vast main portico, where they remain today. The original work was carried out in 1928 by artist Colin Gill. We used old photographs and flakes of paint to restore the colours and decoration to the original, astonishing, effect.

The ceiling of the portico at Blenheim and the recently restored paintings of six disembodied eyes in striking starbursts. The blue eyes are those of Gladys Deacon; the brown eyes are those of the 9th Duke.

Blenheim Art Foundation

This initiative was launched in October 2014 by my half-brother, Edward Spencer-Churchill, with the opening of the inaugural exhibition *Ai Weiwei at Blenheim Palace*, which offered visitors the unique opportunity to experience the work of international contemporary artists within the historic setting of the palace and its grounds. The foundation is a nonprofit organisation that aims to challenge convention and break away from the usual presentation of contemporary art in galleries with bare white walls and no distracting features.

The stated aims of the Blenheim Art Foundation are to show artists most relevant to our time, looking to those who question conventional thinking in contemporary art. Notable artists have included Michelangelo Pistolleto, Lawrence Weiner, Cecily Brown and Maurizio Cattelan, whose renowned gold loo was stolen from the palace in an audacious twilight raid.

above Maurizio Cattelan's fully-functioning gold lavatory pan, entitled *America*.

right Michelangelo Pistoletto's mirrored table and mismatched chairs, *Amar las diferencias*.

following pages Ai Weiwei's *Zodiac Heads*, a recreation in gold of the twelve bronze animal heads that once adorned the Zodiac Fountain in the Old Summer Palace in Beijing.

Public Events

Today we stage annual events that provide entertainment to the general public and the family alike. The Blenheim International Horse Trials, a three-day event established in 1990, has become an important annual event not only within the Blenheim calendar but for the eventing industry, offering European and Olympic riders a first-class, four-star-rated event and a challenging course across our beautiful parkland. Riders compete in tough Dressage, Cross Country and Show Jumping disciplines and the public can enjoy a wide range of hospitality packages and a family day out. It takes place in September.

The very stylish and much-admired Salon Privé, usually held in the last week of August, is one of the world's most prestigious automotive events. The event attracts the most exotic and desirable brands, many of whom attend the event to show off their latest creations. It is the gold standard event for historic cars, with expert judges giving awards in a variety of classes and guests enjoying a top-class hospitality experience.

On a more informal theme, the Nocturne Live concerts, which take place in the North Courtyard over four to five days in June, cater to all ages and music-lovers and offer a memorable evening out, come rain or shine. The first contemporary concert that I remember well was in August 1983, when the legendary Barry Manilow played for 40,000 adoring fans. I think my father loved every minute as much as they did.

previous pages and opposite below The prestigious Salon Privé is an international showcase for car brands and car enthusiasts from all over the globe and it's a great day out.

above The Blenheim International Horse Trials, an annual event that attracts horses and riders of the highest calibre.

opposite above An amazing open-air venue for the massively popular Nocturne Live series of concerts.

Dressed for Christmas

The Christmas Experience at Blenheim has been bringing in huge crowds since 2016. It starts with an illuminated outdoor light trail, and then visitors are treated to an extravagant, themed decoration of the palace. Themes have typically included popular fairy tales such as *Sleeping Beauty*, *Cinderella* and *Alice in Wonderland*. The decoration is carried out by a specialist firm and planned a year in advance.

When my father was still alive, family Christmases at Blenheim were such an iconic highlight of the year, and it is a shame that commercialisation and the lack of family occupying the house has led to the demise of this tradition. But the upside is that the Christmas Experience brings in much-needed revenue for essential restoration projects.

The upside is that the Christmas Experience brings in much-needed revenue for essential restoration projects.

More is more for Christmas at Blenheim, with fairy tales brought magically to life by an amazing team of decorators who dream up a different theme every year: Cinderella's carriage parked in the Great Hall; trees festooned with every bauble in the box; fairy lights and candles; wreaths, garlands, and frosted fruits; ribbons, bows, and golden plates. It is a visual feast not to be missed.

Acknowledgements

The author would like to thank:

My editor and co-author Alexandra Parsons and this will be our twelfth book working together over more than thirty years. She is a huge pleasure to work with, professional, dedicated and has a great sense of humour which is a necessity over a long period of time.

The main photographer, Hugo Rittson-Thomas, who is no stranger to photographing complex projects and over a period of seasons and all times of day. He has a great eye for capturing different angles and details which have been essential for this book.

Pete Seaward, the Blenheim in-house photographer who has huge knowledge of the estate and manages to capture unique images at every occasion and has been invaluable in providing not only additional essential images but superb aerial shots.

Robert Dalrymple, the book designer whose skill at placing and manoeuvring images and text is second to none and achieved at great speed and aplomb.

Many of the Blenheim staff for their knowledge and immense help in sourcing material, providing information on the collections and cooperating with photographic shoots. My particular thanks go to:

Alexa Frost, archivist

Kate Ballenger and Carmen Alvarez, keeper and deputy of the Palace and collections

Robin Wallis, butler, for his expertise and help in setting up table landscapes and room shots

Timothy Mayhew, former butler and a fountain of knowledge of tradition and the family

Mollie Langston, for providing floral arrangements

My huge thanks also to my immediate and extended family and current and future custodians of Blenheim. Particular gratitude to my son David for the thoughtful and evocative foreword.

Lastly huge thanks to my publishers Rizzoli: Charles Miers for persuading me to finally tackle this mammoth task and to Ellen Nidy for her profession-alism and patience in seeing this to fruition.

Index

THE MARLBOROUGH (SPENCE

SIR WINSTON CHURCHILL *b.*1620 *m* ELIZABETH DRAKE of Ashe, Devon

JOHN
*b.*1650, cr. **Duke of Marlborough**° and K.G. 1702
cr. Prince of the Holy Roman Empire 1705
*dspms.*16 June 1722

m SARAH
dr. of Richard
*b.*1660. *m.*167

JOHN
Marquess of Blandford
*b.*1686. *d.*1703

HENRIETTA
*b.*1681. Suc. as **Duchess**
of Marlborough 1722
*dspms.*1733

m FRANCIS
2nd Earl of
Godolphin

ANNE
*b.*1684
*d.*1716

m CHARLES SPENCER K.G.
3rd Earl of Sunderland
*b.*1675 *d.*1722

ELIZA
*b.*168
*d.*171

ROBERT SPENCER
*b.*1701. Suc. as Earl of
Sunderland 1722. *d.*1729

CHARLES SPENCER
*b.*1706. Suc. as Earl of
Sunderland 1729 and as **3rd Duke**
of Marlborough 1733. K.G. *d.*1758

m ELIZABETH
dr. of Lord
Trevor

JOHN SPENCER
*b.*1708 *d.*1746
(Ancestor of the
Earls Spencer)

m GEORGINA CAROLINE CARTERET
dr. of Earl Granville
*b*1716 *d.*1780

GEORGE SPENCER
4th Duke of Marlborough
K.G., L.L.D., F.R.S.
*b.*1739. Suc.1758. *d.*1817

m CAROLINE
dr. of Duke of Bedford
*b.*1743. *d.*1811

GEORGE SPENCER-CHURCHILL†
5th Duke of Marlborough
*b.*1766. Suc. 1817. *d.*1840

m SUSAN
dr. of 7th Earl of Galloway
*b.*1767. *d.*1841

† The 5th Duke was authoris
Churchill, in addition to and after
His Grace's family a surname to v
Duke of Marlborough, added such i

GEORGE SPENCER-CHURCHILL
6th Duke of Marlborough
*b.*1793. Suc. 1840. *d.*1857

m (I) JANE, dr. of 8th Earl of Galloway, *d.*1844
(II) CHARLOTTE, dr. of Viscount Ashbrook, *d.*1850
(III)JANE, dr. of Hon. Edward Stewart, *d.*1897

JOHN WINSTON SPENCER-CHURCHILL *m* FRANCES
7th Duke of Marlborough, K.G.
*b.*1822, M.P. Suc. 1857
Gov. Gen. of Ireland 1876-80, *d.*1883

dr. of Marquess of Londonderry

GEORGE CHARLES SPENCER-CHURCHILL *m* (I) ALBERTHA dr. of Duke of Abercom
8th Duke of Marlborough
*b.*1844. Suc. 1883. *d.*1892

(II) LILIAN dr. of Cicero Price (USA)

CHARLES RICHARD JOHN SPENCER-CHURCHILL *m* (I) CONSUELO dr. of William Vanderbilt (USA)
9th Duke of Marlborough. K.G.
*b.*1871. Suc.1892. *d.*1934

*m.*1895. *d.*1964
(II) GLADYS dr. of Edward Parker Deacon (USA)
*m.*1921. *d.*1977

JOHN ALBERT EDWARD WILLIAM SPENCER-CHURCHILL *m* (I) ALEXANDRA MARY CADOGAN, dr. of Vicount Chelsea,
10th Duke of Marlborough. J.P., D.L.
*b.*1897. Suc. 1934. *d.*1972

*m.*1920. C.B.E., J.P. Chief Comdt. A.T.S. 1938-40. *d.*1961
(II) LAURA, dr. of Hon. Guy Charteris, *m.*1972

IVOR CHARL
*b.*1898. *d.*195

JOHN GEORGE VANDERBILT HENRY
SPENCER-CHURCHILL
11th Duke of Marlborough. J.P., D.L.
*b.*13 April 1926. Suc. 1972. *d.* 2014

m (I) SUSAN MARY, dr. of Michael Hornby, *m.*1951 *d.*2005
(II) ATHINA MARY, dr. of Stavros G. Livanos, *m.*1961
(III) DAGMAR ROSITA dr. of Count Carl Ludwig Douglas, *m.*1972
(IV) LILY MAHTANI, *m.* 2008

CHARLES GEORGE WILLIAM
COLIN SPENCER-CHURCHILL
*b.*1940 *m.* (I) 1965 Gillian Spreckels Fuller
*d.*2016 (II) 1970 Elizabeth Jane Wyndhan
(III) 2014 Sarah Goodbody

SARAH
SPENCER
*b.*1921,
m. (I) 1
(II) 1
(III) 1

JOHN DAVID IVOR
SPENCER-CHURCHILL
*b.*1952. *d.*1955

CHARLES JAMES
SPENCER-CHURCHILL
12th Duke of Marlborough
b. 24 Nov. 1955. Suc. 2014

m (I) REBECCA MARY FEW BROWN *m.*1990
(II) EDLA GRIFFITHS *m.* 2002

HENRIETTA MARY
SPENCER-CHURCHILL
*b.*1958
*m.*1980 Nathan Gelber

RICHARD
SPENCER-CHURCHILL
*b.*1973 *d.*1973

EDWARD
SPENCER-
*b.*1974

GEORGE JOHN GODOLPHIN
SPENCER-CHURCHILL
Marquess of Blandford
b. 28 July 1992

ARAMINTA CLEMENTINE MEGAN
CADOGAN SPENCER-CHURCHILL
b. 2007

CASPAR IVOR ELLIS
SPENCER-CHURCHILL
b. 2008

DAVID ABA GELBER
*b.*1981

MAXIMILL
*b.*1985 *m.* 2